Microcomputer Spreadsheet Models for Libraries

Preparing Documents, Budgets, and Statistical Reports

Philip M. Clark, Ph.D.

American Library Association

Chicago 1985

Designed by Gordon Stromberg

Composed by Impressions, Inc., in
    Palatino and Helvetica on a
    Penta-driven Autologic APS-μ5
    Phototypesetting system

Printed on 55-pound Glatfelter,
    a pH-neutral stock, and bound
    in 10-point Carolina cover stock
    by Cushing-Malloy, Inc.

Library of Congress Cataloging in Publication Data

Clark, Philip M.
    Microcomputer spreadsheet models for libraries.

    Includes index.
        1. Libraries—Automation.   2. Electronic spreadsheets.
3. Microcomputers—Library applications.   4. Library
planning—Data processing.   5. Library finance—Data
processing.   6. Library statistics—Data processing.
I. Title.
Z678.9.C53 1985   025'.0028'54   84–20470
ISBN 0–8389–0403–3

*To the memory of
Ernest R. DeProspo, Jr.*

Contents

1 An Introduction to Electronic Spreadsheets 1

2 Organization, Approach, and Conventions 9

3 Warm-Up Exercises for the Occasional Spreadsheet User 107

Tables

Figures

Preface

This book is devoted to one software application for microcomputers—the electronic spreadsheet. It includes both an introduction to electronic spreadsheet programs for the novice and applications for intermediate and advanced users. The examples are designed for librarians, primarily those who work in public and academic libraries, but the fundamental techniques used to construct the models can be applied to any library, business, school, or home use.

An enormous number of spreadsheet programs is available for microcomputers. Five of the most popular, as of this writing, are VisiCalc, by VisiCorp; SuperCalc, by Sorcim; MultiPlan, by MicroSoft; Perfect Calc, by Perfect Software; and, 1-2-3, by Lotus Development Corporation. VisiCalc was the first spreadsheet program for microcomputers, and contributed enormously to the sales of Apple and Radio Shack micros. SuperCalc improved on the basic concept of VisiCalc and achieved a strong following by being included free with the purchase of the Osborne 1 microcomputer. Perfect Calc has been "bundled" with the purchase of a number of microcomputers, especially the Kaypro micros. MultiPlan and Lotus 1-2-3 have a strong following among owners of IBM-PC micros.

VisiCalc and SuperCalc, often called "first-generation" spreadsheet programs, lack the versatility of the "second generation," such as MultiPlan, Perfect Calc, and Lotus 1-2-3. In fact, Lotus 1-2-3 is more than a spreadsheet program; it includes extensive data management and graphing capabilities as well.

The examples in this book use VisiCalc and SuperCalc as the common denominator; that is, the first-generation spreadsheets. The more flexible and feature-filled second-generation programs can perform all the operations contained in this book with ease. A Command Comparison Guide to the differences in certain basic operations is included in the introductory chapter to assist the users of five different programs in understanding my terminology. I should note that the examples were developed using SuperCalc2 (an enhanced version of SuperCalc) on an Osborne 1 microcomputer, but this in no way precludes users of other programs and other hardware from using this book.

The primary advantage of using an electronic spreadsheet is its computing power. Instead of writing numbers on a piece of paper, numbers are typed into a calculator. This calculator can remember what you told it to do the last time you used it. When you enter a new set of numbers into various places in a spreadsheet, the spreadsheet uses a series of formulas it already knows to make further computations and add the results to the spreadsheet. The spreadsheet may, for example, calculate the totals of rows and columns, calculate percentages, or compare two numbers and select the larger one for further calculation. As a result, updating a report from month to month may require only entering a set of raw numbers; the spreadsheet knows how to compile and prepare them for presentation.

The series of formulas that create the spreadsheet are called *models* or *templates*. Some people use the two terms, *model* and *template*, synonymously. Others object, saying that the two terms are different. I make the following distinction: a *model* is a general approach to a particular problem while a *template* is an exact pattern to be followed.

The spreadsheets in this book are models which will have to be modified to meet your library's particular needs. They probably cannot be used entirely as is. It would be presumptuous of me to suggest that the categories I have chosen for illustration are the only ones applicable to libraries. That presupposes that a standard has been accepted by the field. There are no standards for the type of statistical reporting described in this book.

But the need for some uniformity in reporting is apparent. State, regional, and national agencies and associations need to have a uniform terminology for statistical reporting *and* uniformity in data collection. It is not my purpose to define terms. I assume that you will follow guides such as ALA's *Library Data Collection Handbook*, the ANSI Z39 standards for library statistics, or your state's definition of terms. Further, when conducting data collection exercises such as those proposed by *Output Measures for Public Libraries*, you will collect the data according to the procedures set forth in that book. I provide only the mechanisms for bringing this information together, along with some reasonably simple techniques for the subsequent analysis of the data.

This book contains thirty spreadsheet models with instructions on how the models can be entered on a microcomputer. By no means have I covered all the possible types of models. Rather, I have tried to design models that deal with commonly reported aspects of library service: budgets, expenditures and income, library activity reports. A special section is devoted to *Output Measures for Public Libraries* because experience with measures of this type convinced me that one of the greatest drawbacks to using them is the problem of organizing and analyzing the data collected. Several models will show specific types of formulas, such as "nested IF statements" (which allow complex comparisons to be made automatically) while others are primarily reports rather than calculating models.

Finally, a lengthy section of the book is devoted to models that allow you to analyze data. The collection of factual data, without some analysis and interpretation, is a waste of everyone's time. The models that are presented can assist some readers in exploring the statistical analysis of their data.

To assist the beginning "spreadsheeter" and the occasional user, I have included eight "warm-up exercises." These exercises cover the basic functions used in designing spreadsheets. Most of the spreadsheet programs on the market have additional features that greatly enhance your ability to design a template. By using the functions and features reviewed in the Warm-Up Exercises, you will be able to follow the models I have provided. As mentioned previously, a Command Comparison Guide compares the various commands and functions of the most popular spreadsheets (as of this writing) so that you can translate my terminology to that used by your spreadsheet's creator.

Help, guidance, criticism, and encouragement were received from a great number of people. My wife, Ellen Connor Clark, cleaned up my florid prose and allowed a pervasive intruder, in the form of a microcomputer, into our home. Mary Jo Lynch, director of ALA's Office for Research, was tremendously encouraging from beginning to end. Elaine McConnell provided opportunities to work with her staff at Piscataway (N.J.) Public Library in developing spreadsheet models, and examples of statistical reports. Caroline Coughlin, of Drew University, came through in a pinch with college library statistics forms. Bob Burns, of Colorado State University (a fellow Osborne user), provided valuable technical advice and criticism. Joe Brinley, my editor at ALA, did what a good editor does: encourage, criticize, and revise.

Jim and Barbara Parker of Mid-Coast Microcomputing (in Belfast, Maine) combined the encouragement of old friends with practical assistance on things computing. My summer of writing the beginning draft will long be remembered for their contributions (which ranged from intellectual to liquid). Early on, Barbara Smith of the

Portland (Me.) Public Library faced me with statistical reporting problems that eventually led to this book.

Thanks are also due James Benson, Leny and Jay Struminger, a variety of Osborne users throughout the country, and the faculty, staff, and students at St. John's University (especially those students who contributed by testing the instructions in class exercises). I probably should also thank Adam Osborne, if only because he marketed the first microcomputer I could afford and included two great software programs in the deal: SuperCalc by Sorcim and Wordstar by Micropro.

This book really started in the fall of 1963 when I walked into the Institute of Public Administration at Penn State as a new master's student and met Ernie DeProspo. We worked together for most of the twenty years that followed, until his death in the fall of 1983. Much of that work revolved around statistical reporting systems for libraries and performance measurement. It obviously has influenced this book through the selection of the spreadsheet models that are illustrated.

Ernie was also a dear friend outside the work environment. He and his wife Joyce were like a brother and sister to me, and I deeply appreciate all the warmth and kindness they gave me over the years. This book is dedicated to Ernie in memory of his personal and professional friendship.

1 An Introduction to Electronic Spreadsheets

Anyone in a library who must deal with numbers can benefit from using a spreadsheet program on a microcomputer. But how many librarians deal with numbers? More than you might expect. The obvious "number crunchers" among librarians are those in the administrative offices where payrolls are prepared, expenditures and income accounted for, reports to the board or university officials are developed on library resources and activities, and special studies are conducted. But many department or branch heads submit detailed budget requests, routinely report on circulation, reference and program activity, count use of their services, and study their operations in quantitative terms.

If you use a desk calculator for two hours or more a month, a spreadsheet program can help you. The more you deal with numbers, the more a spreadsheet program becomes a productivity tool, saving you time and energy. Like all tools, you will find new uses for it.

This book attempts to give you a variety of ideas for using spreadsheet programs on microcomputers. Included are examples of budgets, expenditure reports, and daily, monthly, and yearly activity reports, as well as calculation models for conducting special studies and simple models for preparing reports to outside agencies. The examples range from the simple to the complex. Beginners should be able to follow the detailed instructions that are provided with each spreadsheet model. Advanced spreadsheeters will probably bypass the instructions and look instead to the details of formula construction. Whatever your level of sophistication with spreadsheet programs, there should be some idea or hint that will be useful to you.

The examples in this book are partly drawn from real life and partly from my own concerns. I have attempted to give examples that I have seen in use in libraries. In a number of cases, I have kept the detailed categories to a minimum to simplify the beginner's job. Where I have felt detail is necessary, I have included it. Thus some spreadsheet models will fit on a single sheet of paper while others, in printed form, fill two 11-by-15-inch sheets (in small type).

Who Can Use a Spreadsheet Program and for What?

The complexity of some of the formulas should not inhibit you from beginning to learn how to "program" a spreadsheet. The capacity of spreadsheet programs to copy formulas quickly from one place to many other places is one of the major labor-saving attributes of such software.

An Approach to Learning Spreadsheet Design

Before you can begin to design a report or series of calculations using a spreadsheet program, you must learn how to use your program. Eight warm-up exercises presented in part 3 have been designed to help (1) the beginner and (2) the occasional user. These exercises can be used as a tutorial for brushing up on the commands and instructions used by your program. Experienced users of spreadsheet programs will not need these exercises. However, everyone should study the comparison of the command structures (given later) to familiarize themselves with terms I use throughout the book. It has been difficult to try to write for users of the many different brands of spreadsheet programs and thus I have kept the use of commands to a minimum, relying on techniques that can be used with all programs.

What Is a Spreadsheet Program?

The name *spreadsheet* comes from the columnar pads used by accountants, book-keepers, and financial planners. A series of *columns* are arrayed across the top of the page and a series of *rows* are arrayed from top to bottom. The spot where a column and a row intersect is called a *cell*. Electronic spreadsheet programs save formulas for performing calculations in individual cells. The formulas are reused later and do not have to be reentered; this is the first advantage of the spreadsheet.

Table 1 is an example of one portion of a blank spreadsheet. The columns are across the top, ranging from column A through column F. The rows are down the left side and range from row 1 through row 10. You designate a cell by its column and row coordinate so that you can refer to cell A1 or cell E9 and the like.

Table 1. Spreadsheet Matrix

	A	B	C	D	E	F
1						
2						
3						
4						
5						
6						
7						
8						
9						
10						

It must be pointed out that the designation of columns with letters and rows with numbers is *not* uniform among spreadsheet programs. MultiPlan, for example, uses the letter *C* and a number for columns and the letter *R* and a number for rows. Thus cell A5 would be R5C1 in MultiPlan. I have followed the more conventional notation of uppercase letters for columns and numbers for rows.

The first-generation spreadsheet programs allow up to 64 columns and 254 rows if the computer has sufficient memory. The newer programs (including enhanced versions of VisiCalc and SuperCalc) have virtually unlimited numbers of columns and rows.

Electronic spreadsheets allow you to enter text into cells—for example, at the top to show a column heading and on the left to give an explanation of what is in a row. They also allow you to enter numbers into cells that you want to manipulate in some way. Also, you can enter formulas that specify what calculations you want to perform.

An electronic spreadsheet is first and foremost a numerical calculator. (It can perform a variety of mathematical functions that will be explained below.) Second, a series of built-in commands allow you to *edit* what is in the spreadsheet, change the *format* of columns and rows or split the screen into two or more *windows*, *load* or *save* portions or all of the spreadsheet, *print* the spreadsheet or a portion of it, and create for or use data from other types of programs, such as data base managers or word processors. These features vary from one spreadsheet program to another, and only the most common commands will be discussed.

Major Functions of Spreadsheet Programs

Calculator Functions

The four arithmetic operations of addition, subtraction, multiplication, and division are available, together with functions that raise a number to a *power*. The calculator also recognizes relations between numbers, such as "is equal to," "is greater than," etc. By examining such conditions in particular cells, the calculator learns whether or not to perform subsequent operations, defined by the user. In addition, the spreadsheet programs include a number of built-in arithmetic and trigonometric functions, as well as Boolean algebraic functions. But the three built-in functions that you will use most heavily are SUM, COUNT, and AVERAGE.

Table 2 is an example of a spreadsheet with five numbers that are summed, then counted, then averaged. The spreadsheet has also found, in rows 10 and 11, the maximum and minimum of the five numbers, and in row 12 it has found the square root of the number in B7.

The functions SUM, COUNT, AVERAGE, MAX, MIN, and SQRT are followed by the range of cells that you wish to include in calculation. Thus the range in the SUM example in table 2 is from B1 through B5. Or you can specify a particular cell, as in SQRT(B7), where you calculated the square root of the sum of the five numbers from B1 through B5.

The formulas are typed or "entered" in the cell where you wish to have the calculated value appear. Actually, cell B7 in table 2 contains the formula SUM(B1:B5), although it is the result, the number 9923, that appears on the screen or printout in that cell.

Table 2. Spreadsheet Example of Functions and Formulas

	A		B	
1	Number 1		1234	
2	Number 2		4567	
3	Number 3		789	
4	Number 4		2222	
5	Number 5		1111	
6				
7	SUM(B1:B5)		9923	
8	COUNT(B1:B5)		5	
9	AVERAGE(B1:B5)		1984.6	
10	MAX(B1:B5)		4567	
11	MIN(B1:B5)		789	
12	SQRT(B7)		99.61425600786	

Text can also be entered, as well as numbers and formulas. All the entries in column A are actually text entries while column B is composed of either numbers or formulas. Throughout this book I have used the convention of designating a range of values with a colon, as in (B1:B5). In some programs (VisiCalc is an example), the range specification is made with periods, as in (B1. . .B5). Also, some programs require that a function such as SUM or AVERAGE be preceded by a special character, such as @. I have not done so in order to save space and to emphasize the function rather than the input method. *Please check the conventions used with your program when interpreting the formula worksheets that are given throughout this book.*

Several other functions are occasionally used in this book. They include the functions IF, AND, OR, and NOT (OR and NOT are *not* used in this book but are available), as well as the function LOOKUP. These functions will be explained as they appear.

Arithmetic operators can be used within a single cell or in reference to other cells. Within a particular cell, you can construct a series of arithmetic expressions, such as

$$(12+14+6)/2$$

which means add 12, 14, and 6 together, then divide by 2 (the result will be 16).

Placement of parentheses is important, for without them you have a different approach to calculation. Thus, if the expression is changed to

$$12+14+6/2$$

the program will first divide 6 by 2, then add the result (3) to 12 and 14 (the result being 29). Again, you must consult the instruction manual that comes with your spreadsheet program to see the order of calculation with these arithmetic operators.

A formula in a cell can reference different cells as well. The formula

$$(B10-B11)/B8$$

if entered into table 2 means subtract the contents of B11 (the minimum) from the contents of B10 (the maximum) and divide the result by the contents of B8 (the count). Of course, numbers and cell references can be intermixed, such as

$$(435-B8)*2.45$$

meaning subtract the contents of B8 from the number 435 and multiply (indicated by *) the result by 2.45.

What makes electronic spreadsheets so useful is that the formulas can be saved, and when new numbers are entered, recalculation is practically instantaneous. Therefore, a budget spreadsheet can be saved and the following year all you need do is enter the new figures. Calculation takes place instantly.

Command Operations

Operations such as editing, formating, loading and saving, printing, and changing the appearance of the screen allow the spreadsheet to be developed quickly and easily. It is in these areas that the differences between spreadsheet programs are most apparent.

If you are planning to buy a spreadsheet program, consider the following commands to be the minimum that a spreadsheet must have. Within each command, enhancements are available in some programs that are not available in others. Look for these special features and take them into consideration when evaluating a spreadsheet program. They may make your life a lot easier.

BLANK command: Erases the contents of the cell where the *cursor* is located. In some spreadsheet programs, a range of cells can be BLANKed.

CLEAR command: Erases everything on the screen.

DELETE command: Deletes the contents of an entire row or column, then automatically adjusts the formulas in the entire spreadsheet.

EDIT command: Changes previously entered numbers, text, or formulas that are shown on the *entry line* (where the cursor is positioned).

FORMAT command: Allows right or left justification of numbers and/or text; displays numbers as integers, dollar amounts or a specified number of digits, and scientific notation; provides simple graphing of data; and adjusts column width. Some programs allow the formating of individual cells while others are restricted to either columns or rows.

INSERT command: Inserts a new row or column at a designated place.

MOVE command: Moves a row or column to a new position on the spreadsheet.

PRINT command: Prints the spreadsheet or a portion of the spreadsheet on a printer or other device (such as a disk).

REPLICATE command: One of the most often used and valuable features of spreadsheet programs, it allows you to copy a formula or group of formulas to other cells. In the process, the cell references can be automatically changed. Extensive use of this function is made throughout this book.

SAVE and LOAD commands: These commands load a previously prepared spreadsheet from a disk file, and store or save new or revised spreadsheets either in part or in whole. In addition, some can save or load information in the DIF (Data Interchange Format), which allows interaction between certain word processors, database managers, or other spreadsheet programs.

WINDOW command: Splits the screen into two portions, horizontally or vertically, so that widely separated data can be viewed at the same time. You can move from window to window with a simple command.

QUIT command: Stops the operation of the spreadsheet program and exits to the microcomputer's operating system.

GOTO command: Quickly repositions the cursor to any designated portion of the spreadsheet.

RECALCULATE command: Causes the entire spreadsheet to be recalculated. Useful in large spreadsheets when you do not want the spreadsheet recalculated each time you enter a new number.

REPEAT ENTRY command: Copies the contents of one cell down a column or across a row. Used to insert lines to separate portions of the spreadsheet.

START TEXT command: Some spreadsheet programs require that you precede each entry of text with a symbol. Others do not.

START FORMULA command: Some spreadsheet programs require that you precede each entry of a formula with a symbol. Others do not.

HELP command: Shows a variety of screens of advice and assistance, depending on the problem you encounter. Programs vary greatly in the amount of detail these HELP screens contain.

Comparison Guide to Spreadsheet Commands and Functions

The creators of spreadsheet programs that have been marketed since the success of VisiCalc have both improved upon and departed from VisiCalc's original approach.

VisiCalc's advanced version recognizes some of the desired features in its competitor's products.

The models designed for this book assume as a common denominator the level of features such as those in VisiCalc and SuperCalc (not their advanced versions). These are termed *first-generation* spreadsheets and do not have certain formating, data handling, and file manipulation features of the *second-generation* spreadsheets, such as Perfect Calc, MultiPlan, Lotus 1-2-3, and the like. For an excellent comparative review of the features of the most popular spreadsheet programs, read Henderson, Cobb, and Cobb's book *Spreadsheet Software from VisiCalc to 1-2-3* (Indianapolis: Que Corp., 1983).

In the Command Comparison Guide (table 3), I have selected a series of basic operations that will be referred to in the spreadsheet model design section. These basic operations range from BLANKing and CLEARing through the important REPLICATE command. For each of these basic commands I have listed the command sequence that five of the most popular spreadsheet programs use. Obviously, many additional commands are available, such as centering text, calling up data stored in buffers, saving to print files (among others), but I have relied upon these basic commands that can be performed by all the mentioned programs. Therefore, all the spreadsheet models in the pages that follow are capable of being performed with the *first-generation* spreadsheets, as well as the more advanced programs.

The designation of columns and rows differs between spreadsheet programs as well. VisiCalc, SuperCalc, and Lotus 1-2-3 use uppercase letters to designate the columns and numbers to designate the rows. Perfect Calc starts the spreadsheet with columns designated as lowercase letters (*a, b, c,* etc.), then switches to uppercase after *z*. Perfect Calc also uses numbers to designate the rows. MultiPlan has a logical, though different, method of designating columns and rows; all are numbers. Thus column A in VisiCalc would be column 1 in MultiPlan. A cell reference to A1 in VisiCalc would be R1C1 (row 1, column 1) in MultiPlan.

I have used the convention of uppercase letters to designate a column. Perfect Calc users should have little trouble adapting to this notation. MultiPlan users must adapt the formulas in my spreadsheets to their own notation.

In addition to the basic commands, some programs have other features that are very attractive to the spreadsheet designer. A partial list includes

> Commands that protect cells from inadvertent erasure or change
> Commands that sort and merge data
> Global find and replace commands, such as those found on most word
>   processors
> Target seeking
> Title centering
> Pagination
> Special built-in financial functions, such as net present value
> A combination of spreadsheet, word processor, and database manager

Hardware Requirements

Not all spreadsheet programs can be used on all microcomputers. Some are designed for a specific machine while others have versions for a number of different *types* of machines. If you already own a microcomputer, you will be limited to spreadsheet programs that have been created for it. If you have no microcomputer, you have the choice of a variety of spreadsheet programs with a variety of features. Choose the spreadsheet program that has the features you want, then buy the machine that will run your selected program.

In addition to the variety of commands that are available within spreadsheet programs, you must consider the size of the spreadsheets you will want to construct.

Table 3. Command Comparison Guiide to Spreadsheet Programs

BASIC OPERATION	SUPERCALC	VISICALC	MULTIPLAN	PERFECT CALC (C- means CTRL)	LOTUS 1-2-3
BLANK or erase	/B(lank),range	/B(lank)	B(lank)	C-D & ESC D	/R(ange) E(rase)
CLEAR the spreadsheet	/Z(ap)	/C(lear)	T(ransfer) C(lear)	C-X C-K	/W(orksheet) E(rase)
DELETE columns or rows	/D(elete) C,R	/D(elete)	D(elete) C(olumn) or DR	C-C or ESC C	/W(orksheet) D(elete)
EDIT a cell	/E(dit)	/E(dit)	E(dit) A(lpha)	C-XE	F2 (Edit)
Display FORMAT:					
Text right	/F(ormat) T(ext) R(ight)	/F(ormat) R(ight)	F(ormat) R(ight)	C-Xjr	"
Text left	/F(ormat) T(ext) L(eft)	/F(ormat) L(eft)	F(ormat) L(eft)	C-Xjl	'
NO decimals	/F(ormat) I(nteger)	/FI(nteger)	F(ormat) I(nteger)	C-Xd0	/R(ange) F(ormat) F(ixed) 0
TWO decimals	/F(ormat) $(dollar)	F$	F(ormat) $	C-Xd$	/R(ange) F(ormat) C(ents)
Column width	/F(ormat) 0-127	/G(lobal) C(olumns)	F(ormat)D(efault)W(idth)	C-XW	/W(orksheet) C(olumn) W(idth)
INSERT columns or rows	/I(nsert) C,R	/I(nsert) C,R	I(nsert)C,R	C-O or ESC O	/W(orksheet) I(nsert)
MOVE columns or rows	/M(ove) C,R	/M(ove) C,R	M(ove),C,R	ESC W C-Y	/M(ove)
PRINT	/O(utput)	/P(rint)	P(rint)	C-X C-P	/P(rint)
REPLICATE:					
Many to many	/C(opy)	/R(eplicate)	C(opy)F(rom)	ESC W C-Y	/C(opy)
One to many	/R(eplicate)	/R(eplicate)	C(opy)R(ight) or D(own)	C-W ESC Y	/C(opy)
LOAD a file	/L(oad) A(ll) P(art)	/S(torage)L(oad)	T(ransfer)L(oad)	C-X C-F or C-R	/F(ile) R(etrieve)
SAVE a file	/S(ave) A(ll) P(art)	/S(torage)S(ave)	T(ransfer)S(ave)	C-X C-S or C-W	/F(ile) S(ave)
QUIT (exit to system)	/Q(uit)	/S(torage)Q(uit)	Q(uit)	C-X C-C	/Q(uit)
WINDOW split	/W(indow) H(oriz),V(ert)	/W(indow)	W(indow)S(plit)	C-X2	/W(orksheet) W(indow)
GOTO row–col.	=	>	Goto	>	F5 (GoTo)
Next window	;		F1 (Next Window)	C-Xo	F6 (Next Window)
Recalculate	!	....	F4 (Recalculate)	!	
REPEAT ENTRY	"	/-	REPT	ESC W C-Y	
Start text				=	
Start formula		@		?	
HELP	?	?			F1

Memory limitations can prevent you from designing the type of spreadsheet you might wish. While most spreadsheets offer a matrix of 64 columns and 254 rows, not all of the matrix can be accessed with particular microcomputers. For example, the Osborne I microcomputer that was used to write this book has 64K RAM, but the maximum memory that can be used to store a spreadsheet in SuperCalc is 27K. Thus a spreadsheet of 30 columns and 150 rows is about the maximum that could be accessed by that machine. Hardware constraints, rather than the program itself, limit some spreadsheets.

Starting to Use a Spreadsheet Program

The first thing to learn about your spreadsheet program is how information is displayed on the screen. All the programs have an *entry line* which shows what you are typing and where it will be entered into a particular location. Some indicate where the *cursor* will go to after you enter text or numbers; others do not. On some spreadsheet programs, you will be shown the amount of space remaining (or used), which is helpful in determining how much larger your spreadsheet can be.

Of greatest importance is the designation of a *filename*. You will want to save your spreadsheet model on a disk and retrieve it later. Therefore, it needs a name that you can refer to. The length of a filename will depend on your microcomputer's operating system, but generally, names up to eight characters are permitted.

It is helpful to include a filename on every spreadsheet you create. It is also helpful to indicate when you created the spreadsheet and when you last entered or changed it. The examples in this book contain space in the first three rows for this information, as well as room to place additional information such as your name, instructions for using the spreadsheet, etc.

Planning and Organizing a Spreadsheet

A general rule for using all spreadsheet programs is to locate the information in the top-left portion of the spreadsheet. Many programs allocate memory based on the number of cells that are above and to the left of the entry farthest from the upper-left corner. They do this even if nothing is located in those cells! Therefore, use empty cells sparingly if you are working on a large spreadsheet.

You may want to do a rough design of your spreadsheet with paper and pencil before you actually start to enter text and numbers. As you become familiar with the commands for moving, inserting, deleting, and formating, you will probably "design" on the screen itself. Especially at the beginning of your experience with a spreadsheet, however, block out what will go where.

Most programs have *default* format settings for text and numbers. Text is usually "left justified" and numbers are "right justified." The appearance of a report is important. I have used a general approach of "right" justifying text in columns of numbers. Also, I have usually kept all text in column A "left" justified, purely for appearance sake. You may wish to do the same.

The addition of horizontal lines to delineate sections of the report also helps to increase the visual impact. The REPEAT ENTRY command is used extensively in the examples to create these lines.

Finally, you are able to print portions of spreadsheets. Thus you do not need to include in your printout the filename designation or instructions that you might have placed in the upper rows. If you can print a report without the column and row designations at the top and left side, the attractiveness of the report is enhanced.

2 Organization, Approach, and Conventions

The approach to discussion of each of the thirty spreadsheet models that follow is to (1) introduce the concept or problem that the model addresses, (2) point out the general design features of the model, such as unusual formulas that are used, (3) list specific steps to be taken in entering text and formulas (on a column-by-column basis), and (4) where applicable, discuss how you might go about actually using the model once you have created it.

Two illustrations accompany each discussion of a model. The first illustration is the appearance of the completed spreadsheet after you have entered both the formulas and your data. The second illustration is the critical one. It lists all the formulas used to create the model. This *formula worksheet* resembles a regular spreadsheet, except that formulas appear where there would be numbers were you using (rather than creating) the spreadsheet.

In the illustrations, the numbers or "data" that appear are products of my imagination; they are not real. In using the spreadsheet models, you will have to change these data to reflect the activity that your library experiences. You can use my numbers to check to see if you have made any errors in entering formulas. But eventually you will want to erase my example data. (People who have tested these spreadsheet models generally liked having the example data on the formula worksheet so that they could check for errors.)

In the detailed descriptions that follow (of how to create each spreadsheet), practically all references to the illustrations are to the formula worksheets. When I refer to, for example, the Budget model, I am usually calling your attention to something on the formula worksheet. In fact, the illustration that precedes the discussion is merely to show you what a completed spreadsheet would look like; it is essentially worthless as a guide to creating the spreadsheet.

Each spreadsheet model is referred to by its *filename*; a short title of eight or fewer characters. You will want to create your own filenames to indicate more precisely the subject and date of the model. For example, BUD84-1 could indicate that this is your budget for 1984, first version. Or ACT0385 could mean a library activity report for March 1985. You will have to be inventive in creating filenames if you are limited to an eight-character string.

Many of the example spreadsheets display dollar signs ($) and commas separating numbers (e.g., 123,456). Columns, rows, and even groups of cells can be formated by some spreadsheet programs to insert these signs. Percentage signs (%) are also capable of being inserted by some programs and the decimal point moved to the appropriate place. I have included the dollar signs and the commas for the sake of appearance, but if your spreadsheet program does not allow such formating, be advised that your spreadsheet will not look like my examples.

The complexity of the formulas in these models ranges from simple addition through the use of multiple functions within a single formula. I have deliberately tried to introduce a variety of types of formulas throughout the examples in order that you may see how formulas are actually used. Most tutorials that come with spreadsheet programs do not include this type of detail; such detail is included in this book to allow you to move beyond the simple functions that spreadsheet programs allow.

While many of the examples deal with public libraries, the formula construction details will be of interest to academic and other librarians. And several models that use academic statistics as their base will be of interest to public librarians because of the formulas that are used.

Table 4 is a list of the models in this book, with my rating of their complexity. I have given three ratings: *novice*, for the beginning user; *intermediate*, for those who have mastered the *novice* models; and, *advanced*, for either its special applications or for the complexity of the formulas in the model. In addition, I have listed some of the major functions performed by the formulas as a type of index for finding specific applications.

Summary of Conventions Used in This Book

Part 1, An Introduction to Electronic Spreadsheets, contains a number of warnings about the conventions I have used in this book concerning cell designations, range specifications, command differences between spreadsheet programs, etc. The major conventions I have used are briefly summarized below. For more detail, see especially the section that contains the Command Comparison Guide (page 7).

Capital letters in formulas refer to columns and numbers designate rows (i.e., in a cell reference A5, the *A* is for column A and the *5* is for row 5.

Range designations are indicated by a colon (:), as in A5:F5 (referring to the range of cells from A5 through F5). Several spreadsheet programs use a series of dots (. . .) to specify a range, as in A5. . .F5.

COPY and REPLICATE commands vary greatly from program to program. I can only repeat that you should consult your program instructional manual to learn the exact procedure you must follow.

The designation of a formula entry also varies greatly from program to program. Several programs (such as VisiCalc and Lotus 1-2-3) require that you precede a formula beginning with an alphabetic character with either an "at" sign (@) or a math symbol (+). Due to the diversity of approaches, I have not included such initial symbols.

Table 4. Complexity and Features of the Spreadsheet Models

Filename	Rating	Features
BUDGET	*Novice*	Percentaging
EXPEND	*Novice*	Year to date, File transfer
DISBMO	*Intermediate*	IF statement to transfer data
ACTIVDAY	*Novice*	SUM, AVERAGE, MAX, MIN, COUNT
ACTIVMO	*Novice*	Spreadsheet consolidation
ACTIVYR	*Novice*	Spreadsheet consolidation
ACTIVCL	*Novice*	Year to date, File transfer
COLLECT	*Novice*	File transfer
PAY	*Advanced*	IF with LOOKUP, LOOKUP
CJFORM	*Novice*	Allocation model
VOIGT	*Advanced*	Nested IF statements, If with LOOKUP
INLIB	*Advanced*	IF, SUM, AVERAGE
VISITS	*Novice*	Simple math
PROGRAM	*Novice*	COUNT, SUM, AVERAGE
REFER	*Novice*	SUM, Percentaging
MATER	*Intermediate*	SUM, COUNT, Percentaging, Survey question tabulation
OPMSUM	*Novice*	A report form
DSTAT	*Intermediate*	COUNT, SUM, AVERAGE, MAX, MIN, SQRT
CORREG	*Advanced*	Very complex formulas
FREQ	*Intermediate*	IF statements
GROUP	*Intermediate*	Special use of LOOKUP
CONTIN	*Advanced*	AND statement
XTAB	*Advanced*	Statistical analysis
LQ	*Advanced*	Statistical analysis
SSIZE	*Intermediate*	LOOKUP
HEGIS	*Novice*	Form transfer
HEGISAID	*Advanced*	Nested IF statements
PLSTAT	*Novice*	Form transfer
ARLSTAT	*Novice*	Form transfer

Tools for Budgets, Expenditures, Library Activities, and Collection Evaluation

BUDGET: A Public Library Expense Budget

The preparation of the annual budget is a chore that faces all public and academic library directors. While there are a number of different types of budget statements and processes, ranging from the line-item budget to the zero-based budgeting system popularized by the Carter administration in the 1970s, the illustration used here is the commonly used line-item or object-of-expenditure budget.

Budget preparation typically involves a series of steps, beginning with initial estimates and eventually evolving into a final document that is presented to the governing authorities. While the basic items of expenditure usually do not change from one time to another, the amounts do, and it is at these points that the electronic spreadsheet begins to earn its keep. Once the model has been constructed, new amounts can be entered and the revised budget is immediately available. The new budget can be printed and distributed quickly, without waiting for a typist to revise what is a difficult typing job.

General Design Features

Looking at figure 1, the example spreadsheet, you can see that the Budget model contains three major expense categories: Salaries and Wages, Library Materials, and Other Expenses. Detailed expense items for each of the three categories are subentries. More or less detail may be necessary in your library, but this example is fairly typical.

Usually, decision makers want to compare the requested budget with the previous year's budget. The Budget model is designed to provide that comparison, both in terms of the actual dollar difference (column H) and the percentage difference between the two years (column I). The percentages in columns E and G show the percentage that each item contributes to the total for that year.

Text and Formula Entry (Use figure 2, Formula Worksheet)

Columns A, B, and C; Width = 12, Text Left

Enter the filename and other text, using the space provided in the three columns. The subcategories of expenses can be indented by starting in column B.

The long lines in rows 4, 9, and 40 can be entered by using the REPEAT ENTRY function, found in most spreadsheet programs.

Columns D through I; Width = 12, Text Right

Enter the column headings in rows 7 and 8.

```
 !  A  !!  B  !!  C  !!  D  !!  E  !!  F  !!  G  !!  H  !!  I  !
 1 ! Filename:                    BUDGET
 2 ! Date Created:
 3 ! Date Last Changed:
 4 ! =============================================================
 5 !                   EXPENSE BUDGET - 1984
 6 !
 7 !                   1983      1983      1984      1984    $ DIFF    % DIFF
 8 ! EXPENSES          BUDGET   PERCENT   REQUEST  PERCENT  1983-1984 1983-1984
 9 ! - - - - - - - - - - - - - - - - - - - - - - - - - - - - - - -
10 ! Salaries and Wages:
11 !     Professional  $143,000   31.64   $158,000   31.32   $15,000    10.49
12 !     Clerical      $125,000   27.66   $137,000   27.16   $12,000     9.60
13 !     Janitorial     $45,000    9.96    $47,000    9.32    $2,000     4.44
14 !     Subtotal: S & W $313,000  69.25   $342,000   67.79   $29,000     9.27
15 !     Benefits       $14,000    3.10    $16,000    3.17    $2,000    14.29
16 !
17 ! Library Materials:
18 !     Books          $45,925   10.16    $50,500   10.01    $4,575     9.96
19 !     Periodicals     $5,780    1.28     $5,200    1.03     $-580   -10.03
20 !     Audiovisual     $3,650     .81     $4,650     .92     $1,000    27.40
21 !     Subtotal: Materials $55,355 12.25  $60,350   11.96    $4,995     9.02
22 !
23 ! Other Expenses:
24 !     Public Programs  $1,450    .32     $2,650     .53     $1,200    82.76
25 !     Postage          $1,600    .35     $2,000     .40      $400     25.00
26 !     Mileage            $950    .21     $1,095     .22      $145     15.26
27 !     Bookmobile Maintenance $2,200 .49  $2,200     .44       $0       .00
28 !     Janitorial Supplies $850   .19     $2,000     .40     $1,150   135.29
29 !     Library Supplies   $5,500  1.22     $8,000    1.59     $2,500    45.45
30 !     Conferences/Dues   $1,200   .27     $1,500     .30      $300     25.00
31 !     Maintenance of Buildings
32 !        and Grounds     $3,600   .80     $4,400     .87      $800     22.22
33 !     Utilities         $34,850  7.71    $51,670   10.24   $16.820    48.26
34 !     Building Rental    $8,000  1.77        $0      .00   $-8,000  -100.00
35 !     Service of Equipment $1,900 .42     $2,800     .56      $900     47.37
36 !     Professional Services $945  .21       $600     .12     $-345   -36.51
37 !     Equipment Purchase  $6,166 1.36     $6,797    1.35      $631     10.23
38 !     Miscellaneous        $400   .09       $400     .08       $0       .00
39 !     Subtotal: Other Expenses $69,611 15.40 $86,112 17.07  $16,501    23.70
40 ! - - - - - - - - - - - - - - - - - - - - - - - - - - - - - - -
41 ! Grand Total        $451,966  100.00  $504,462  100.00   $52,496    11.62
42 !
```

Figure 1. BUDGET:
Public Library Expense
Budget, Example
Spreadsheet

Column D
   There are three subtotal formulas and one grand total formula in this
   column, as well as some financial data that I have invented. (You do
   not have to enter the financial data unless you wish to check your
   work with mine.) Use the SUM function of your spreadsheet program
   to calculate the four totals.
   The formulas in column F perform the same function as those in
   column D. COPY or REPLICATE the four formulas in column D to
   column F.
   REPLICATE the formula in cell D41 to cells E41 through H41. You
   may find that this type of SUM operation does not work on your
   spreadsheet program and that you will have to change the formula to
   D14+D15+D21+D39. Both formulas produce the same result.
Column E
   Percentaging is performed by dividing an entry by the total of all the
   entries. In cell E11, you will divide the Professional Salaries figure

	A	B	C	D	E	F	G	H	I
1	Filename:								
2	Date Created:								
3	Date Last Changed:								
4	=========								
5									
6									
7				EXPENSE BUDGET – 1984					
8	EXPENSES			1983 BUDGET	1983 PERCENT	1984 REQUEST	1984 PERCENT	$ DIFF 1983–1984	% DIFF 1983–1984
9									
10	Salaries and Wages:								
11	Professional			143000	D11/D41*100	158000	F11/F41*100	F11-D11	(F11-D11)/D11*100
12	Clerical			125000	D12/D41*100	137000	F12/F41*100	F12-D12	(F12-D12)/D12*100
13	Janitorial			45000	D13/D41*100	47000	F13/F41*100	F13-D13	(F13-D13)/D13*100
14	Subtotal: S & W			SUM(D11:D13)		SUM(F11:F13)	F14/F41*100	F14-D14	(F14-D14)/D14*100
15	Benefits			14000	D15/D41*100	16000	F15/F41*100	F15-D15	(F15-D15)/D15*100
16									
17	Library Materials:								
18	Books			45925	D18/D41*100	50500	F18/F41*100	F18-D18	(F18-D18)/D18*100
19	Periodicals			5780	D19/D41*100	5200	F19/F41*100	F19-D19	(F19-D19)/D19*100
20	Audiovisual			3650	D20/D41*100	4650	F20/F41*100	F20-D20	(F20-D20)/D20*100
21	Subtotal: Materials			SUM(D18:D20)		SUM(F18:F20)	F21/F41*100	F21-D21	(F21-D21)/D21*100
22									
23	Other Expenses:								
24	Public Programs			1450	D24/D41*100	2650	F24/F41*100	F24-D24	(F24-D24)/D24*100
25	Postage			1600	D25/D41*100	2000	F25/F41*100	F25-D25	(F25-D25)/D25*100
26	Mileage			950	D26/D41*100	1095	F26/F41*100	F26-D26	(F26-D26)/D26*100
27	Bookmobile Maintenance			2200	D27/D41*100	2200	F27/F41*100	F27-D27	(F27-D27)/D27*100
28	Janitorial Supplies			850	D28/D41*100	2000	F28/F41*100	F28-D28	(F28-D28)/D28*100
29	Library Supplies			5500	D29/D41*100	8000	F29/F41*100	F29-D29	(F29-D29)/D29*100
30	Conferences/Dues			1200	D30/D41*100	1500	F30/F41*100	F30-D30	(F30-D30)/D30*100
31	Maintenance of Buildings								
32	and Grounds			3600	D32/D41*100	4400	F32/F41*100	F32-D32	(F32-D32)/D32*100
33	Utilities			34850	D33/D41*100	51670	F33/F41*100	F33-D33	(F33-D33)/D33*100
34	Building Rental			8000	D34/D41*100	0	F34/F41*100	F34-D34	(F34-D34)/D34*100
35	Service of Equipment			1900	D35/D41*100	2800	F35/F41*100	F35-D35	(F35-D35)/D35*100
36	Professional Services			945	D36/D41*100	600	F36/F41*100	F36-D36	(F36-D36)/D36*100
37	Equipment Purchase			6166	D37/D41*100	6797	F37/F41*100	F37-D37	(F37-D37)/D37*100
38	Miscellaneous			400	D38/D41*100	400	F38/F41*100	F38-D38	(F38-D38)/D38*100
39	Subtotal: Other Expenses			SUM(D24:D38)	D39/D41*100	SUM(F24:F38)	F39/F41*100	SUM(H24:H38)	(F39-D39)/D39*100
40									
41	Grand Total			SUM(D14,D15,D21,D39)	SUM(E14,E15,E21,E39)	SUM(F14,F15,F21,F39)	SUM(G14,G15,G21,G39)	SUM(H14,H15,H21,H39)	(F41-D41)/D41*100
42									

Figure 2. BUDGET: Public Library Expense Budget, Formula Worksheet

(contained in D11) by the Grand Total that is in D41. If your
spreadsheet allows an automatic movement of the decimal point two
spaces to the right, use that function. If not, multiply by 100 to move
the decimal point two places to the right.
REPLICATE the formula in cell E11 to cells E12 through E39. You
must be careful to specify that you do *not* want to change the reference
to D41 in the formula.
COPY or REPLICATE the formulas in column E to column G, as they
are the same.
Column H
The formulas are a simple subtraction of the amounts entered in
column D from column F. Enter the subtraction formula in cell H11
and REPLICATE it to H12 through H39.
Column I
To find the percentage difference between the two years, you can use
the difference calculated in column H and divide by the earliest year—
in this case the amount in column D. Multiplying by 100 moves the
decimal point the needed two places to the right, if necessary.
REPLICATE the formula in cell I11 to cells I12 through I41.

You can now clean up the spreadsheet by blanking the entries in rows 16, 17,
22, 23, and 31 for columns D through I.

Using the Model

You may change any of the amounts in column F to see the impact on the total
and the differences between the years. You can eliminate unwanted categories of expenditures or add additional categories. A final printed report need not include the
first four rows of the spreadsheet, which are internal information.

EXPEND: A Library Expenditure Status Report (figure 3)

Monthly expenditure reports are prepared by librarians in order to account for
the funds entrusted to them, as well as for management decision making. Perhaps the
most necessary item of information as the fiscal year nears its end is the balance
remaining in various budget categories.

General Design Features

The Expend model is an example of a typical end of the month report of expenditures for the year-to-date (YTD), the current month, and the balance remaining.
The approved budget for the year is presented and, based on the expenditures to date,
a calculation is made of the balance in dollars and the percent of the budget that
remains. Each line-item entry is given an *object code number* in column A as a form of
shorthand for the entry.
The model relies on information stored in the previous month's report in order
to update the YTD this-month column. Depending on the spreadsheet program you
are using, this transfer process from one spreadsheet to another will be somewhat
complicated or quite simple. (Use Warm-Up Exercise 7, part 3, to practice the transfer
process.)

	A	B	C	D	E	F	G	H	I
1	Filename:								
2	Date Created:								
3	Date Last Changed:		EXPEND						
5	LIBRARY BUDGET STATUS REPORT FOR MONTH OF:								
7	OBJECT		DESCRIPTION	ANNUAL	Y-T-D	EXPENDITURES	Y-T-D	BALANCE	PERCENT
8	CODE			BUDGET	PRIOR MONTH	THIS MONTH	THIS MONTH		REMAINING
10	101		Executive Salaries	$40,850.00	$13,616.00	$3,404.00	$17,020.00	$23,830.00	58
11	102		Instructional Sal - F/T	$336,900.00	$112,300.00	$28,075.00	$140,375.00	$196,525.00	58
12	103		Non-Instructional Sal - F/T	$16,800.00	$5,600.00	$1,400.00	$7,000.00	$9,800.00	58
13	104		Non-Instructional Sal - P/T	$800.00	$156.00		$156.00	$644.00	81
14	105		Tech/Clerical Sal - F/T	$130,048.00	$43,349.00	$10,837.00	$54,186.00	$75,862.00	58
15	106		Tech/Clerical Sal - P/T	$59,186.00	$19,854.00	$4,128.56	$23,982.56	$35,203.44	59
16	107		Student Employees	$103,985.00	$25,750.00	$9,363.97	$35,113.97	$68,871.03	66
18	100		Total - Personnel	$688,569.00	$220,625.00	$57,208.53	$277,833.53	$410,735.47	60
20	201		Departmental Allocations	$35,900.00	$12,125.00	$8,582.57	$20,707.57	$15,192.43	42
21	202		General Reference	$26,500.00	$8,500.00	$2,196.64	$10,696.64	$15,803.36	60
22	203		Microforms	$8,600.00	$2,550.00	$65.38	$2,615.38	$5,984.62	70
23	204		Periodical Subscriptions	$44,000.00	$42,691.31	$350.76	$43,042.07	$957.93	2
25	200		Total - Library Materials	$115,000.00	$65,866.31	$11,195.35	$77,061.66	$37,938.34	33
27	301		Travel	$2,050.00	$451.06	$551.37	$1,002.43	$1,047.57	51
28	302		Postage and Freight	$2,000.00	$298.37	$402.52	$700.89	$1,299.11	65
29	303		Phone Expense	$700.00	$77.95	$80.92	$158.87	$541.13	77
30	304		Photo Duplication	$900.00	$103.56	$29.06	$132.62	$767.38	85
31	305		Maintenance Contracts	$6,380.00	$5,800.00	$125.85	$5,925.85	$454.15	7
32	306		Equipment	$2,000.00	$1,200.00	$325.00	$1,525.00	$475.00	24
33	307		Office Material & Supplies	$5,000.00	$2,200.00	$265.00	$2,465.00	$2,535.00	51
34	308		Data Base Searching	$6,000.00	$2,050.00	$206.93	$2,256.93	$3,743.07	62
35	309		OCLC	$33,000.00	$17,565.00	$2,750.00	$20,315.00	$12,685.00	38
36	310		Miscellaneous	$1,400.00	$72.93	$308.86	$381.79	$1,018.21	73
38	300		Total - Other Expenses	$59,430.00	$29,818.87	$5,045.51	$34,864.38	$24,565.62	41
40			Grand Total	$862,999.00	$316,310.18	$73,449.39	$389,759.57	$473,239.43	55

Figure 3. EXPEND: Library Expenditure Status Report, Example Spreadsheet

Text and Formula Entry (See figure 4, Formula Worksheet)

Columns A, B, and C; Width = 15, Text Left

> Enter the text as given in the three columns provided. The long lines in rows 4, 9, and 39 can be drawn by using the REPEAT ENTRY function found in most spreadsheet programs.

Columns D through I; Width = 15, Text Right

> Enter the column headings in rows 7 and 8.

Column D

> The approved annual budget amounts should be entered in the first month of the fiscal year. Normally they will remain the same for the remainder of the year, but they can be adjusted if necessary. If adjustments will be made, enter the SUM formulas where indicated. REPLICATE the grand total formula in D38 to F38 through H38.

Column E

> All the amounts in this column will be transferred from the previous month's report. No formulas should be placed in this column.

Column F

> Four SUM formulas are shown for this column. If the amounts are to be shown to the cent, format this column and columns G and H to two decimal places.

Column G

> The simple addition of the entries in columns E and F results in the YTD this-month calculation. REPLICATE the formula in G10 to G11 through G38.

Column H

> Balance-remaining is a simple subtraction of the expenditures to date (column G) from the annual budget (column D). REPLICATE the formula in H10 to H11 through H38.

Column I

> The percent-remaining calculation is performed by dividing the balance in column H by the annual budget in column D. Multiplying by 100 moves the decimal point two places to the right. REPLICATE the formula in I10 to I11 through I40. In order to show no decimal places for the percent figure, format column I to INTEGER.

You may now clean up the spreadsheet by blanking or erasing the entries in rows 17, 19, 24, 26, and 37.

Using the Model

In the first month of the fiscal year, you will not have to transfer the information for YTD prior-month (column E) because there have been no expenditures for the year as yet. But, beginning with the second month, you will have to transfer the contents of column G to column E.

This transfer process can be performed in two general ways. First, you can start with a blank copy of the model that contains only the formulas and the annual budget figures. Then load the part of the previous month's spreadsheet that you need (column G) into column E of this month's spreadsheet. Then enter the expenditures for this month in column F, and the remaining columns will be calculated.

Second, if your spreadsheet is capable of replicating only the values (i.e., the actual amounts) from one column to another, you can take a copy of the previous month's spreadsheet, REPLICATE the values in column G to column E, and enter the

	A	B	C	D	E	F	G	H	I
1	Filename:		EXPEND						
2	Date Created:								
3	Date Last Changed:								
4	===	===	===	===	===	===	===	===	===
5	LIBRARY BUDGET STATUS REPORT FOR MONTH OF:								
6									
7	OBJECT	DESCRIPTION		ANNUAL	Y-T-D	EXPENDITURES	Y-T-D	BALANCE	PERCENT
8	CODE			BUDGET	PRIOR MONTH	THIS MONTH	THIS MONTH		REMAINING
9	---	---		---	---	---	---	---	---
10	101	Executive Salaries		40850	13616	3404	E10+F10	D10-G10	H10/D10 * 100
11	102	Instructional Sal - F/T		336900	112300	28075	E11+F11	D11-G11	H11/D11 * 100
12	103	Non-Instructional Sal - F/T		16800	5600	1400	E12+F12	D12-G12	H12/D12 * 100
13	104	Non-Instructional Sal - P/T		800	156		E13+F13	D13-G13	H13/D13 * 100
14	105	Tech/Clerical Sal - F/T		130048	43349	10837	E14+F14	D14-G14	H14/D14 * 100
15	106	Tech/Clerical Sal - P/T		59186	19854	4128.56	E15+F15	D15-G15	H15/D15 * 100
16	107	Student Employees		103985	25750	9363.97	E16+F16	D16-G16	H16/D16 * 100
17									
18	100	Total - Personnel		688569	220625	SUM(F10:F16)	E18+F18	D18-G18	H18/D18 * 100
19									
20	201	Departmental Allocations		35900	12125	8582.57	E20+F20	D20-G20	H20/D20 * 100
21	202	General Reference		26500	8500	2196.64	E21+F21	D21-G21	H21/D21 * 100
22	203	Microforms		8600	2550	65.38	E22+F22	D22-G22	H22/D22 * 100
23	204	Periodical Subscriptions		44000	42691.31	350.76	E23+F23	D23-G23	H23/D23 * 100
24									
25	200	Total - Library Materials		115000	65866.31	SUM(F20:F23)	E25+F25	D25-G25	H25/D25 * 100
26									
27	301	Travel		2050	451.06	551.37	E27+F27	D27-G27	H27/D27 * 100
28	302	Postage and Freight		2000	298.37	402.52	E28+F28	D28-G28	H28/D28 * 100
29	303	Phone Expense		700	77.95	80.92	E29+F29	D29-G29	H29/D29 * 100
30	304	Photo Duplication		900	103.56	29.06	E30+F30	D30-G30	H30/D30 * 100
31	305	Maintenance Contracts		6380	5800	125.85	E31+F31	D31-G31	H31/D31 * 100
32	306	Equipment		2000	1200	325	E32+F32	D32-G32	H32/D32 * 100
33	307	Office Material & Supplies		5000	2200	265	E33+F33	D33-G33	H33/D33 * 100
34	308	Data Base Searching		6000	2050	206.93	E34+F34	D34-G34	H34/D34 * 100
35	309	OCLC		33000	17565	2750	E35+F35	D35-G35	H35/D35 * 100
36	310	Miscellaneous		1400	72.93	308.86	E36+F36	D36-G36	H36/D36 * 100
37									
38	300	Total - Other Expenses		59430	29818.87	SUM(F27:F36)	E38+F38	D38-G38	H38/D38 * 100
39									
40		Grand Total		862999	316310.18	F18+F25+F38	G18+G25+G38	H18+H25+H38	H40/D40 * 100

Figure 4. EXPEND: Library Expenditure Status Report, Formula Worksheet

new Expenditures for This Month in column F. With this method, be sure to update *all* the numbers in column F (Expenditures This Month)—that is, show a zero if no expenditure is made—because you do not want to have one of last month's expenditures shown for this month. A better solution is to blank or erase all the data entries in column F (but not the formulas) and then enter this month's figures.

To retain a copy of each month's report, SAVE the new file under a unique filename. If they are monthly reports, use an abbreviated month name appended to the regular filename. For example, EXPJAN might indicate that this is the expenditure report for January.

The basis for a simple bookkeeping system can be found in the DISBMO spreadsheet. In the example given (see figure 5), you have both a check register (i.e., a list of all checks you write) and the posting of each check to its respective line-item account. By changing the column headings in rows 7 and 8 to reflect income sources, two of the major elements of a bookkeeping system are in place.

The DISBMO formula worksheet (figure 6) illustrates the valuable use of the IF statement to post the check amounts to the account columns. While the formula worksheet looks formidable, formula entry is not complicated due to the availability of the REPLICATE command in spreadsheet programs.

DISBMO: A Monthly Cash Disbursements Journal

General Design Features

The left-hand portion of the spreadsheet from column A through column F constitutes a check register. The date, check number, description, account code (more on this later), and the amount are placed in the appropriate columns. The formulas that contain IF statements automatically post the amount you place in column F into the proper column. The columns are then summed, resulting in the total expenditures to date for each expenditure category.

The key to this transfer process is the account code in column E. You must decide what type of expenditure this check represents and place the proper code in column E. The IF statements match the number in column F with the numbers in row 6, columns G through N. When the two agree, the amount is copied to that location.

Here is how you read the IF statements that are on the formula worksheet. The IF statement in cell G10 is

$$IF(E10 = G6, F10, 0)$$

This says that if the account code number in cell E10 is exactly the same as the number in cell G6, copy the amount of the check that is found in cell F10 to this location, which is cell G10. If the numbers in E10 and G6 do not match, place a zero in this location.

For the first check that is listed (number 401), the account code is 3, which indicates that the payment is for library materials. The match between the 3 in cell E10 is found with the 3 in row 6 (column I) and thus the amount of $10,050.00 is copied to cell I10.

This technique is used in other spreadsheets in this book and, once learned, has numerous applications in spreadsheet design.

The design that is illustrated allows for only 8 different account codes and a total of 15 checks. These can be expanded to more accounts and more checks, depending on the total allowable size of your spreadsheet program.

							1	2	3	4	5	6	7	8
	A	B	C	D	E	F	Personnel	Benefits	Library Materials	Library Supplies	Buildings & Grounds	Equipment	Contractual Services	Other
1	Filename:		DISBMO											
2	Date Created:													
3	Date Last Changed:													
5	DISBURSEMENTS FOR MONTH OF:													
7	Date	Check Number	Description		Account Code	Amount								
10	4-1	401	Book jobber		3	$10,050.00			$10,050.00					
11	4-1	402	XYZ Publications		3	$12.50			$12.50					
12	4-5	403	Ace Hardware		5	$95.67					$95.67			
13	4-6	404	OCLC		7	$2,343.00							$2,343.00	
14	4-6	405	Computer store		6	$100.00						$100.00		
15	4-6	406	Fuel oil		5	$1,313.00					$1,313.00			
16	4-15	407	Payroll (4-1/4-15)		1	$3,456.00	$3,456.00							
17	4-15	408	Soc Sec		2	$345.00		$345.00						
18	4-16	409	NILA advance		8	$125.00								$125.00
19	4-20	410	Consultant		7	$350.00							$350.00	
20	4-20	411	Window washing		5	$125.00					$125.00			
21	4-20	412	Book jackets		4	$225.50				$225.50				
22	4-20	413	Data base searching		7	$450.00							$450.00	
23	4-20	414	Audit expense		8	$2,200.00								$2,200.00
24	4-30	415	Payroll (4/16-4/30)		1	$3,575.00	$3,575.00							
27	Total Expenditures					$24,765.67	$7,031.00	$345.00	$10,062.50	$225.50	$1,533.67	$100.00	$3,143.00	$2,325.00

Figure 5. DISBMO: Monthly Cash Disbursements Journal, Example Spreadsheet

20

Text and Formula Entry (use figure 6, Formula Worksheet)

Columns A through D; Width = 15, Text Left

Enter the text in columns A, B, and C. The check number can be entered either as a "value" or as a piece of text (a label in some spreadsheets).

Use the REPEAT ENTRY function to place the long lines in rows 4, 9, and 26. The short lines in row 26, columns F through N, will be inserted later.

Columns E through N; Width = 15, Text Right

Enter the numbers 1 through 8 in row 6, beginning at column G and going through column N. These must be entered as values and not as text.

Enter the column headings in rows 7 and 8.

Column E

The numbers in this column will be the codes you assign to your checks. If you want to test your spreadsheet, use the numbers provided and see if the resulting spreadsheet matches the example.

Column F

The only formula is that in cell F27, which SUMs all the checks that have been written. REPLICATE the formula in cell F27 to G27 through N27.

Enter a series of dashes in cell F26 as text. Then REPLICATE cell F26 to G26 through N26.

Column G

Now for the first of the IF statements. Place the formula IF(E10=G6,F10,0) in cell G10.

REPLICATE the formula in G10 to G11 through G25. When replicating, make sure that the reference to cell G6 *does not change*!

Column H

Follow the directions for Column G, but use this formula: IF(E10=H6,F10,0). Remember, H6 *does not change*!

Column I

Follow the directions for Column G, but use this formula: IF(E10=I6,F10,0). Remember, I6 *does not change*!

Column J

Follow the directions for Column G, but use this formula: IF(E10=J6,F10,0). Remember, J6 *does not change*!

Column K

Follow the directions for Column G, but use this formula: IF(E10=K6,F10,0). Remember, K6 *does not change*!

Column L

Follow the directions for Column G, but use this formula: IF(E10=L6,F10,0). Remember, L6 *does not change*!

Column M

Follow the directions for Column G, but use this formula: IF(E10=M6,F10,0). Remember, M6 *does not change*!

Column N

Follow the directions for Column G, but use this formula: IF(E10=N6,F10,0). Remember, N6 *does not change*!

Using the Model

You will want one spreadsheet for each month. Devise a series of filenames (such as DISBJAN, DISBFEB, and so on), in which you will save the month's entries.

	A	B	C	D	E	F	G	H
							1	2
1	Filename:							
2	Date Created:							
3	Date Last Changed:							
4	===							
5	DISBURSEMENTS FOR MONTH OF:							
6								
7	Date	Check Number	Description		Account Code	Amount	Personnel	Benefits
8								
9								
10	4-1	401	Book jobber		3	10050	IF(E10=G6,F10,0)	IF(E10=H6,F10,0)
11	4-1	402	XYZ Publications		3	12.50	IF(E11=G6,F11,0)	IF(E11=H6,F11,0)
12	4-5	403	Ace Hardware		5	95.67	IF(E12=G6,F12,0)	IF(E12=H6,F12,0)
13	4-6	404	OCLC		7	2343	IF(E13=G6,F13,0)	IF(E13=H6,F13,0)
14	4-6	405	Computer store		6	100	IF(E14=G6,F14,0)	IF(E14=H6,F14,0)
15	4-6	406	Fuel oil		5	1313	IF(E15=G6,F15,0)	IF(E15=H6,F15,0)
16	4-15	407	Payroll (4-1/4-15)		1	3456	IF(E16=G6,F16,0)	IF(E16=H6,F16,0)
17	4-15	408	Soc Sec		2	345	IF(E17=G6,F17,0)	IF(E17=H6,F17,0)
18	4-16	409	NJLA advance		8	125	IF(E18=G6,F18,0)	IF(E18=H6,F18,0)
19	4-20	410	Consultant		7	350	IF(E19=G6,F19,0)	IF(E19=H6,F19,0)
20	4-20	411	Window washing		5	125	IF(E20=G6,F20,0)	IF(E20=H6,F20,0)
21	4-20	412	Book jackets		4	225.50	IF(E21=G6,F21,0)	IF(E21=H6,F21,0)
22	4-20	413	Data base searching		7	450	IF(E22=G6,F22,0)	IF(E22=H6,F22,0)
23	4-20	414	Audit expense		8	2200	IF(E23=G6,F23,0)	IF(E23=H6,F23,0)
24	4-30	415	Payroll (4/16-4/30)		1	3575	IF(E24=G6,F24,0)	IF(E24=H6,F24,0)
25							IF(E25=G6,F25,0)	IF(E25=H6,F25,0)
26								
27	Total Expenditures					SUM(F10:F26)	SUM(G10:G26)	SUM(H10:H26)

C: DISBMO

	I	J	K	L	M	N
		3	4	5	6	7	8

	I	J	K	L	M	N
	Library Materials	Library Supplies	Buildings & Grounds	Equipment	Contractual Services	Other
10	IF(E10=I6,F10,0)	IF(E10=J6,F10,0)	IF(E10=K6,F10,0)	IF(E10=L6,F10,0)	IF(E10=M6,F10,0)	IF(E10=N6,F10,0)
11	IF(E11=I6,F11,0)	IF(E11=J6,F11,0)	IF(E11=K6,F11,0)	IF(E11=L6,F11,0)	IF(E11=M6,F11,0)	IF(E11=N6,F11,0)
12	IF(E12=I6,F12,0)	IF(E12=J6,F12,0)	IF(E12=K6,F12,0)	IF(E12=L6,F12,0)	IF(E12=M6,F12,0)	IF(E12=N6,F12,0)
13	IF(E13=I6,F13,0)	IF(E13=J6,F13,0)	IF(E13=K6,F13,0)	IF(E13=L6,F13,0)	IF(E13=M6,F13,0)	IF(E13=N6,F13,0)
14	IF(E14=I6,F14,0)	IF(E14=J6,F14,0)	IF(E14=K6,F14,0)	IF(E14=L6,F14,0)	IF(E14=M6,F14,0)	IF(E14=N6,F14,0)
15	IF(E15=I6,F15,0)	IF(E15=J6,F15,0)	IF(E15=K6,F15,0)	IF(E15=L6,F15,0)	IF(E15=M6,F15,0)	IF(E15=N6,F15,0)
16	IF(E16=I6,F16,0)	IF(E16=J6,F16,0)	IF(E16=K6,F16,0)	IF(E16=L6,F16,0)	IF(E16=M6,F16,0)	IF(E16=N6,F16,0)
17	IF(E17=I6,F17,0)	IF(E17=J6,F17,0)	IF(E17=K6,F17,0)	IF(E17=L6,F17,0)	IF(E17=M6,F17,0)	IF(E17=N6,F17,0)
18	IF(E18=I6,F18,0)	IF(E18=J6,F18,0)	IF(E18=K6,F18,0)	IF(E18=L6,F18,0)	IF(E18=M6,F18,0)	IF(E18=N6,F18,0)
19	IF(E19=I6,F19,0)	IF(E19=J6,F19,0)	IF(E19=K6,F19,0)	IF(E19=L6,F19,0)	IF(E19=M6,F19,0)	IF(E19=N6,F19,0)
20	IF(E20=I6,F20,0)	IF(E20=J6,F20,0)	IF(E20=K6,F20,0)	IF(E20=L6,F20,0)	IF(E20=M6,F20,0)	IF(E20=N6,F20,0)
21	IF(E21=I6,F21,0)	IF(E21=J6,F21,0)	IF(E21=K6,F21,0)	IF(E21=L6,F21,0)	IF(E21=M6,F21,0)	IF(E21=N6,F21,0)
22	IF(E22=I6,F22,0)	IF(E22=J6,F22,0)	IF(E22=K6,F22,0)	IF(E22=L6,F22,0)	IF(E22=M6,F22,0)	IF(E22=N6,F22,0)
23	IF(E23=I6,F23,0)	IF(E23=J6,F23,0)	IF(E23=K6,F23,0)	IF(E23=L6,F23,0)	IF(E23=M6,F23,0)	IF(E23=N6,F23,0)
24	IF(E24=I6,F24,0)	IF(E24=J6,F24,0)	IF(E24=K6,F24,0)	IF(E24=L6,F24,0)	IF(E24=M6,F24,0)	IF(E24=N6,F24,0)
25	IF(E25=I6,F25,0)	IF(E25=J6,F25,0)	IF(E25=K6,F25,0)	IF(E25=L6,F25,0)	IF(E25=M6,F25,0)	IF(E25=N6,F25,0)
27	SUM(I10:I26)	SUM(J10:J26)	SUM(K10:K26)	SUM(L10:L26)	SUM(M10:M26)	SUM(N10:N26)

Figure 6. DISBMO: Monthly Cash Disbursements Journal, Formula Worksheet

When you start a new month, load a copy of the spreadsheet model, blank or erase all the entries from cells A10 through F25, and you will have a blank spreadsheet.

As mentioned earlier, you can change the column headings for this basic model to headings that indicate sources of income. For example, Personnel could be changed to Municipal Appropriation, Benefits could be changed to State Aid, and so forth. Obviously, "Check Number" would be meaningless for income sources, and you can either eliminate column B or leave it blank.

DISBYR: A Month-by-Month Summary of Cash Disbursements

You will probably want a month-by-month summary of your cash disbursements, which you record by using the previous spreadsheet DISBMO. The summary spreadsheet, figure 7, provides that information—and a running total of expenditures as well.

General Design Features

Most of this spreadsheet can be constructed from DISBMO. The easiest approach is to take a copy of one of your DISBMO spreadsheets and do the following:

1. Erase or delete rows 10 through 27. In effect, keep only the heading information.
2. Delete columns C, D, and E. What was column F will now be column C (i.e., the "Amount" column is now column C).
3. Replace the heading "Date" in A7 with the heading "Month." Replace the heading "Check Number" in B7 and B8 with the heading "Filename" in B7.
4. Starting with row 10 in column A, enter the months of the year down to cell A21.
5. Draw some lines in row 23 in columns C through K.
6. SUM each of the columns from C through K in row 23.
7. AVERAGE each column from C through K in row 24. At the end of the year, this will show you the average expenditures per month. (Please note that you must enter zeros when you have not made an expenditure in a category; otherwise, the monthly average will be in error.)

All you need do after you have constructed this model is transfer the contents of row 27 in DISBMO to their appropriate position on this new spreadsheet, named DISBYR. When copying information from one spreadsheet to another, be sure that you transfer only the "values" and not the formulas. You have changed the spreadsheet quite a bit and the old formulas will not work. Obviously, you can also transfer the monthly data to the DISBYR spreadsheet manually, but, if possible, try to use the transfer features of your spreadsheet. (See Warm-Up Exercise 7 for practice in transferring data from one spreadsheet to another.)

ACTIVDAY: A Daily Library Activity Data Entry Form

Circulation activity is one of the statistics most often collected by librarians, but additional statistics are also collected, including counts of reference activity, attendance, programs held and numbers attending, and patrons registered and withdrawn.

The ACTIVDAY spreadsheet is designed to be a *daily* data entry form. Thus there is a record of circulation and information activity for each day that the library is open. While the example spreadsheet (figure 8) does not show all the days in a month, the

	A	B	C	D	E	F	G	H	I	J	K
				1	2	3	4	5	6	7	8
1	Filename:		DISBYR								
2	Date Created										
3	Date Last Changed:										
4											
5	CASH DISBURSEMENT SUMMARY FOR YEAR OF:										
6											
7	Month	Filename	Total Disbursed	Personnel	Benefits	Library Materials	Library Supplies	Buildings & Grounds	Equipment	Contractual Services	Other
8											
9											
10	January	DISBJAN	$32,000.00	$26,000.00	$1,500.00	$1,500.00	$1,000.00	$2,000.00	$.00	$.00	$.00
11	February	DISBFEB	$33,500.00	$26,500.00	$1,500.00	$2,500.00	$.00	$1,900.00	$500.00	$.00	$600.00
12	March	DISBMAR	$33,500.00	$27,000.00	$1,500.00	$3,000.00	$.00	$1,800.00	$200.00	$.00	$.00
13	April	DISBAPR	$41,000.00	$27,500.00	$3,000.00	$3,500.00	$200.00	$1,700.00	$100.00	$3,000.00	$2,000.00
14	May										
15	June										
16	July										
17	August										
18	September										
19	October										
20	November										
21	December										
22											
23	Total to Date		$140,000.00	$107,000.00	$7,500.00	$10,500.00	$1,200.00	$7,400.00	$800.00	$3,000.00	$2,600.00
24	Average to Date		$35,000.00	$26,750.00	$1,875.00	$2,625.00	$300.00	$1,850.00	$200.00	$750.00	$650.00

Figure 7. DISBYR: Month-by-Month Summary of Cash Disbursements, Example Spreadsheet

	A	B	C	D	E	F	G	H	I	J	K	L	M
1:	Filename:		ACTIVDAY										
2:	Date Created:												
3:	Date Last Changed:												
5:	DAILY LIBRARY ACTIVITY ENTRY FORM				ADULT MATERIAL								
6:	MONTH OF:	January											
8:	STATISTICAL		MONTH	MONTH	AVERAGE	HIGHEST	LOWEST						
9:	CATEGORIES		TOTAL	PERCENT	PER DAY	DAY	DAY	Jan 3	Jan 4	Jan 5	Jan 6	Jan 7	Jan 9
11:	CIRCULATION ACTIVITY:												
12:	Non-Fiction		2,826	44.10	113	172	33	101	102	33	151	154	127
13:	Fiction		1,669	26.05	67	129	35	51	62	35	94	86	71
14:	Other Material:												
15:	Cassettes		3	.05	0	1	0	0	0	0	0	0	0
16:	Posters		5	.08	0	1	0	0	0	0	0	0	0
17:	Magazines		506	7.90	20	44	4	12	24	10	26	23	23
18:	Paperbacks		1,098	17.13	44	94	1	80	94	23	46	49	57
19:	Films		42	.66	2	9	0	0	3	2	0	3	0
20:	Records		259	4.04	10	35	3	3	11	14	19	13	10
21:	Other		0	.00	0	0	0	0	0	0	0	0	0
23:	Subtotal: Other		1,913	29.85	77	132	8	95	132	49	91	88	90
25:	Total Circulation		6,408	100.00	256	402	117	247	296	117	336	328	288
27:	INFORMATION ACTIVITY:												
28:	Reference Questions		1,719		69	102	40	75	83	45	90	85	70
29:	Directional Questions		1,825		73	105	45	80	85	50	100	90	75
30:	Attendance		4,268		171	268	78	164	197	78	224	218	192
31:	Programs Held		17		1	2	0	1	1	2	1	1	0
32:	Program Attendance		311		12	52	0	15	15	35	18	14	0
33:	Borrowers Registered		3		0	1	0	0	0	1	0	0	0
34:	Borrowers Withdrawn		56		2	23	0	0	0	18	0	0	0
35:	Hours Open		280		11	12	9	12	12	12	12	9	10
36:	Days Open		25										

Figure 8. ACTIVDAY: Daily Library Activity Data Entry Form, Example Spreadsheet

formulas for the spreadsheet allow you to construct a report that holds up to 31 days of data.

As in other spreadsheets, the statistical categories may be changed to meet your reporting needs. You may wish to report in more detail on fiction and nonfiction, or include expanded definitions of reference activity. I have included a category "Hours Open" with the thought that some libraries might wish to calculate activity by the hour.

General Design Features

The ACTIVDAY spreadsheet calculates the total activity for the month, together with the percentages for circulation activity, and calculates the average activity per day as well as the highest and lowest activity days of the month. The spreadsheet functions AVERAGE, MAX, and MIN are used to calculate these statistics.

If you keep separate statistics on children and young-adult activities, you must prepare another spreadsheet (like this one) to record that activity. (The next spreadsheet, ACTIVMO, allows you to merge the data from both spreadsheets into a library system total for the reporting month. Then, the ACTIVYR spreadsheet summarizes the activity for all the months of the year.)

Text and Formula Entry (See figure 9, Formula Worksheet)

Columns A and B; Width = 12, Text Left

Enter the text as given in the formula worksheet. The indented text is entered in two ways: by inserting several spaces before typing the text and by entering text in column B rather than column A. Enter the long lines in rows 4, 7, and 10 by using the REPEAT ENTRY function of your spreadsheet.

Columns C through AL; Width = 12, Text Right

The column designation AL refers to the 38th column on your spreadsheet. If column A is the first column and column Z is the 26th, some spreadsheet programs begin relettering with AA, AB, and so forth. Thus AL would be the 38th column (26 plus 12).

Enter the column headings in rows 8 and 9. You must change the dates, depending on the month you are working on. Start with the first reporting day in the month in column H and continue, column by column, until all the reporting days are entered. If you wish, you can enter these heading dates as you enter the daily data.

Column C

This column maintains a running total of all activity as you enter each day's data. At the end of the month, this column contains the total activity for the month.

Enter the formula in cell C12 and REPLICATE it to C13 through C35. The formula used to compute the number of days your library was open in the month counts the number of entries in row 35 from column H through column AL (the "Hours Open" row). The COUNT function counts a cell if it has any entry in it, even a zero. Therefore, if you are not open on a particular day, do not enter a zero in row 35. Enter several dashes in cell C22 and REPLICATE the cell to D22 through AL22.

Column D

This column calculates the percentage that each circulation activity category is of the total circulation. Enter the formula in cell D12.

	A	B	C	D	E	F	G	H	I	J	K	L	M
1:	Filename:	ACTIVDAY											
2:	Date Created:												
3:	Date Last Changed:												
4:													
5:	DAILY LIBRARY ACTIVITY ENTRY FORM				ADULT MATERIAL								
6:	MONTH OF:	January											
7:													
8:	STATISTICAL		MONTH	MONTH	AVERAGE	HIGHEST	LOWEST						
9:	CATEGORIES		TOTAL	PERCENT	PER DAY	DAY	DAY	Jan 3	Jan 4	Jan 5	Jan 6	Jan 7	Jan 9
10:													
11:	CIRCULATION ACTIVITY:												
12:	Non-Fiction		SUM(H12:AL12)	C12/C25*100	AVERAGE(H12:AL12)	MAX(H12:AL12)	MIN(H12:AL12)	101	102	33	151	154	127
13:	Fiction		SUM(H13:AL13)	C13/C25*100	AVERAGE(H13:AL13)	MAX(H13:AL13)	MIN(H13:AL13)	51	62	35	94	86	71
14:	Other Material:												
15:	Cassettes		SUM(H15:AL15)	C15/C25*100	AVERAGE(H15:AL15)	MAX(H15:AL15)	MIN(H15:AL15)	0	0	0	0	0	0
16:	Posters		SUM(H16:AL16)	C16/C25*100	AVERAGE(H16:AL16)	MAX(H16:AL16)	MIN(H16:AL16)	0	0	0	0	0	0
17:	Magazines		SUM(H17:AL17)	C17/C25*100	AVERAGE(H17:AL17)	MAX(H17:AL17)	MIN(H17:AL17)	12	24	10	26	23	23
18:	Paperbacks		SUM(H18:AL18)	C18/C25*100	AVERAGE(H18:AL18)	MAX(H18:AL18)	MIN(H18:AL18)	80	94	23	46	49	57
19:	Films		SUM(H19:AL19)	C19/C25*100	AVERAGE(H19:AL19)	MAX(H19:AL19)	MIN(H19:AL19)	0	3	2	0	0	0
20:	Records		SUM(H20:AL20)	C20/C25*100	AVERAGE(H20:AL20)	MAX(H20:AL20)	MIN(H20:AL20)	3	11	14	19	13	10
21:	Other		SUM(H21:AL21)	C21/C25*100	AVERAGE(H21:AL21)	MAX(H21:AL21)	MIN(H21:AL21)	0	0	0	0	0	0
22:													
23:	Subtotal: Other		SUM(H23:AL23)	C23/C25*100	AVERAGE(H23:AL23)	MAX(H23:AL23)	MIN(H23:AL23)	SUM(H15:H21)	SUM(I15:I21)	SUM(J15:J21)	SUM(K15:K21)	SUM(L15:L21)	SUM(M15:M21)
24:													
25:	Total Circulation		SUM(H25:AL25)	C25/C25*100	AVERAGE(H25:AL25)	MAX(H25:AL25)	MIN(H25:AL25)	H12+H13+H23	I12+I13+I23	J12+J13+J23	K12+K13+K23	L12+L13+L23	M12+M13+M23
26:													
27:	INFORMATION ACTIVITY:												
28:	Reference Questions		SUM(H28:AL28)		AVERAGE(H28:AL28)	MAX(H28:AL28)	MIN(H28:AL28)	75	83	45	90	85	70
29:	Directional Questions		SUM(H29:AL29)		AVERAGE(H29:AL29)	MAX(H29:AL29)	MIN(H29:AL29)	80	85	50	100	90	75
30:	Attendance		SUM(H30:AL30)		AVERAGE(H30:AL30)	MAX(H30:AL30)	MIN(H30:AL30)	164	197	78	224	218	192
31:	Programs Held		SUM(H31:AL31)		AVERAGE(H31:AL31)	MAX(H31:AL31)	MIN(H31:AL31)	1	1	2	1	1	0
32:	Program Attendance		SUM(H32:AL32)		AVERAGE(H32:AL32)	MAX(H32:AL32)	MIN(H32:AL32)	15	15	35	18	14	0
33:	Borrowers Registered		SUM(H33:AL33)		AVERAGE(H33:AL33)	MAX(H33:AL33)	MIN(H33:AL33)	0	0	1	0	0	0
34:	Borrowers Withdrawn		SUM(H34:AL34)		AVERAGE(H34:AL34)	MAX(H34:AL34)	MIN(H34:AL34)	0	0	18	0	0	0
35:	Hours Open		SUM(H35:AL35)		AVERAGE(H35:AL35)	MAX(H35:AL35)	MIN(H35:AL35)	12	12	12	12	9	10
36:	Days Open		COUNT(H35:AL35)										

Figure 9. ACTIVDAY: Daily Library Activity Data Entry Form, Formula Worksheet

REPLICATE the formula in cell D12 to D13 through D25, but be sure that the reference to cell C25 in the formula is *not* changed.
Multiplying by 100 moves the decimal point two places to the right.
Column E
This column calculates the mean or AVERAGE for the data entered to date. Enter the formula in cell E12 and REPLICATE it to E13 through E35.
Column F
This column finds the highest number in the row. The function MAX (maximum), which is used in the formula, should be entered in cell F12 and REPLICATED to F13 through F35.
Column G
This column finds the lowest number in the row. The function MIN (minimum), which is used in the formula, should be entered in cell G12 and REPLICATED to G13 through G35.
Column H
This column begins the daily entry portion of the spreadsheet. Place the two formulas in rows 23 and 25 and REPLICATE each to columns I through AL.

Clean up the spreadsheet by blanking or erasing the formulas in rows 14, 24, 26, and 27.

Using the Model

Enter each day's activity in the appropriate column. You will want to set your spreadsheet to "manual calculation" to speed up data entry as you get into the month.

For an end-of-the-month report, print only a portion of the spreadsheet, such as rows 5 through 35 and columns A through G.

You might use some of the statistical spreadsheets elsewhere in this book to analyze the daily library activity. For example, you could analyze the correlation between fiction and nonfiction circulation or the relationship between reference and directional questions.

ACTIVMO: A Monthly Library Activity Summary Report

After you have designed ACTIVDAY, the daily report, you can construct a spreadsheet like ACTIVMO (figure 10). In this case, I have assumed that you will have two daily entry forms: one for adult activity and one for juvenile activity. If you have multiple outlets such as branches and bookmobiles, you will want to design a spreadsheet that shows the activity for each outlet and calculates a system total. By following the directions for ACTIVMO, you should be able to modify it easily to summarize outlet activity rather than adult/juvenile activity.

General Design Features

Unless this is one of your first spreadsheets, you will find the formulas and text entry to be quite simple. The spreadsheet takes information recorded on other spreadsheets (ACTIVDAY for adult and for juvenile activity) and inserts the data in their proper columns. Summing and percentaging are then calculated by ACTIVMO.

Figure 10. ACTIVMO: Monthly Library Activity Summary Report, Example Spreadsheet

	A	B	C	D	E	F	G	H
1	Filename:		ACTIVMO					
2	Date Created:							
3	Date Last Changed:							
4	==							
5	MONTHLY LIBRARY ACTIVITY SUMMARY REPORT							
6	MONTH OF:		January					
7	– –							
8	STATISTICAL		ADULT	ADULT	JUVENILE	JUVENILE	LIBRARY	LIBRARY
9	CATEGORIES		TOTAL	PERCENT	TOTAL	PERCENT	TOTAL	PERCENT
10	....							
11	CIRCULATION ACTIVITY:							
12		Non-Fiction	2,800	44.76	3,000	51.90	5,800	48.19
13		Fiction	1,700	27.18	1,500	25.95	3,200	26.59
14		Other Material:						
15		Cassettes	5	.08	50	.87	55	.46
16		Posters	10	.16	25	.43	35	.29
17		Magazines	500	7.99	250	4.33	750	6.23
18		Paperbacks	1,000	15.99	500	8.65	1,500	12.46
19		Films	40	.64	80	1.38	120	1.00
20		Records	200	3.20	350	6.06	550	4.57
21		Other	0	.00	25	.43	25	.21
22			-----	-----	-----	-----	-----	-----
23		Subtotal: Other	1,755	28.06	1,280	22.15	3,035	25.22
24								
25		Total Circulation	6,255	100.00	5,780	100.00	12,035	100.00
26								
27	INFORMATION ACTIVITY:							
28		Reference Questions	1,800		250		2,050	
29		Directional Questions	3,500		500		4,000	
30		Attendance	5,000		4,000		9,000	
31		Programs Held	20		50		70	
32		Program Attendance	500		600		1,100	
33		Borrowers Registered	25		50		75	
34		Borrowers Withdrawn	10		25		35	
35		Hours Open	250		250			
36		Days Open	25		25			

Text and Formula Entry (See figure 11, Formula Worksheet)

Columns A and B; Width = 12, Text Left

Rather than reenter the text in these two columns, take a copy of ACTIVDAY and delete all the columns but A and B. Or, if you can LOAD a part of a spreadsheet, LOAD only columns A and B.

Columns C through H; Width = 12, Text Right

Enter the long lines in rows 4, 7, and 10 with the REPEAT ENTRY function.

Enter the column headings in rows 8 and 9.

Column C through F

There are no formulas in these columns because it is assumed that you will transfer the values from the total and percent columns in ACTIVDAY to this location. You may do this transfer manually or you may use the capabilities of your spreadsheet program to do the transfer for you. If the program does the transfer, remember to transfer only the values and not the formulas. To practice this type of transfer with your program, see Warm-Up Exercise 7 (in part 3).

Column G

Add the adult total to the juvenile total to arrive at a library total. REPLICATE the formula in cell G12 to G13 through G34. Do not add the "hours open" or the "days open" categories, because to do so would give a false impression.

	A	B	C	D	E	F	G	H	
1	Filename:		ACTIVMO						
2	Date Created:								
3	Date Last Changed:								
4	==								
5	MONTHLY LIBRARY ACTIVITY SUMMARY REPORT								
6	MONTH OF:		January						
7	– –								
8	STATISTICAL		ADULT	ADULT	JUVENILE	JUVENILE	LIBRARY	LIBRARY	
9	CATEGORIES		TOTAL	PERCENT	TOTAL	PERCENT	TOTAL	PERCENT	
10	....								
11	CIRCULATION ACTIVITY:								
12	Non-Fiction		2800	44.76	3000	51.90	C12+E12	G12/G25 * 100	
13	Fiction		1700	27.18	1500	25.95	C13+E13	G13/G25 * 100	
14	Other Material:								
15	Cassettes		5	.08	50	.87	C15+E15	G15/G25 * 100	
16	Posters		10	.16	25	.43	C16+E16	G16/G25 * 100	
17	Magazines		500	7.99	250	4.33	C17+E17	G17/G25 * 100	
18	Paperbacks		1000	15.99	500	8.65	C18+E18	G18/G25 * 100	
19	Films		40	.64	80	1.38	C19+E19	G19/G25 * 100	
20	Records		200	3.20	350	6.06	C20+E20	G20/G25 * 100	
21	Other		0	.00	25	.43	C21+E21	G21/G25 * 100	
22			-----	-----	-----	-----	-----	-------	
23	Subtotal: Other		1755	28.06	1280	22.15	C23+E23	G23/G25 * 100	
24									
25	Total Circulation		6255	100.00	5780	100.00	C25+E25	G25/G25 * 100	
26									
27	INFORMATION ACTIVITY:								
28	Reference Questions		1800		250		C28+E28		
29	Directional Questions		3500		500		C29+E29		
30	Attendance		5000		4000		C30+E30		
31	Programs Held		20		50		C31+E31		
32	Program Attendance		500		600		C32+E32		
33	Borrowers Registered		25		50		C33+E33		
34	Borrowers Withdrawn		10		25		C34+E34		
35	Hours Open		250		250				
36	Days Open		25		25				

Figure 11. ACTIVMO: Monthly Library Activity Summary Report, Formula Worksheet

Column H
Use the formula to calculate the percent of the library total. Enter the formula in cell H12 and REPLICATE it to H13 through H25, making sure the reference to cell G25 *does not change*.

Clean up the spreadsheet by blanking the formulas in rows 24, 26, and 27.

Using the Model

As mentioned earlier, transfer the end-of-the-month total from ACTIVDAY to the appropriate place on ACTIVMO.

ACTIVYR: A Yearly Library Activity Summary Report

There are any number of different spreadsheet summaries that can be prepared using ACTIVDAY, the daily library activity entry form. ACTIVMO is one example, as is the present one, ACTIVYR (figure 12).

In ACTIVYR, you can assemble the monthly activity reports into one combined report and calculate the activity for the entire year. In addition, you can calculate the per capita ratio of activity to the population of your jurisdiction.

	A	B	C	D	E	F	G	H	I	J	K	L	M	N	O	P
1	Filename:		ACTIVYR													
2	Date Created:															
3	Date Last Changed:															
4																
5	YEARLY LIBRARY ACTIVITY SUMMARY REPORT															
6	YEAR OF:					Enter Jurisdiction Population In Cell G6	12,000									
7																
8	STATISTICAL			JAN TOTAL	FEB TOTAL	MAR TOTAL	APR TOTAL	MAY TOTAL	JUNE TOTAL	JULY TOTAL	AUG TOTAL	SEPT TOTAL	OCT TOTAL	NOV TOTAL	DEC TOTAL	1984 TOTAL / PER CAPITA TOTAL
9	CATEGORIES															
10																
11	CIRCULATION ACTIVITY:															
12	Non-Fiction			2,800	2,900	3,000	2,800	2,900	3,000	2,800	2,900	3,000	2,800	2,900	3,000	34,800 / 2.90
13	Fiction			1,700	1,800	1,900	1,700	1,800	1,900	1,700	1,800	1,900	1,700	1,800	1,900	21,600 / 1.80
14	Other Material:															
15	Cassettes			5	10	15	5	10	15	5	10	15	5	10	15	120 / .01
16	Posters			10	15	20	10	15	20	10	15	20	10	15	20	180 / .02
17	Magazines			500	600	700	500	600	700	500	600	700	500	600	700	7,200 / .60
18	Paperbacks			1,000	1,100	1,200	1,000	1,100	1,200	1,000	1,100	1,200	1,000	1,100	1,200	13,200 / 1.10
19	Films			40	50	60	40	50	60	40	50	60	40	50	60	600 / .05
20	Records			200	300	400	200	300	400	200	300	400	200	300	400	3,600 / .30
21	Other			0	10	20	0	10	20	0	10	20	0	10	20	120 / .01
22																
23	Subtotal: Other			1,755	2,085	2,415	1,755	2,085	2,415	1,755	2,085	2,415	1,755	2,085	2,415	25,020 / 2.09
24																
25	Total Circulation			6,255	6,785	7,315	6,255	6,785	7,315	6,255	6,785	7,315	6,255	6,785	7,315	49,740 / 4.15
26																
27	INFORMATION ACTIVITY:															
28	Reference Questions			1,800	1,900	2,000	1,800	1,900	2,000	1,800	1,900	2,000	1,800	1,900	2,000	22,800 / 1.90
29	Directional Questions			3,500	3,600	3,700	3,500	3,600	3,700	3,500	3,600	3,700	3,500	3,600	3,700	43,200 / 3.60
30	Attendance			5,000	5,500	6,000	5,000	5,500	6,000	5,000	5,500	6,000	5,000	5,500	6,000	66,000 / 5.50
31	Programs Held			20	30	40	20	30	40	20	30	40	20	30	40	360
32	Program Attendance			500	550	600	500	550	600	500	550	600	500	550	600	6,600
33	Borrowers Registered			25	30	35	25	30	35	25	30	35	25	30	35	360
34	Borrowers Withdrawn			10	15	20	10	15	20	10	15	20	10	15	20	180
35	Hours Open			250	300	350	250	300	350	250	300	350	250	300	350	3,600
36	Days Open			25	25	25	25	25	25	25	25	25	25	25	25	300

Figure 12. ACTIVYR: Yearly Library Activity Summary Report, Example Spreadsheet

General Design Features

As in ACTIVMO, this spreadsheet is constructed by transferring portions of AC-TIVDAY to ACTIVYR. The text in columns A and B remains the same. The total activity column is transferred each month to this new spreadsheet. The only formulas in the spreadsheet are found in columns O and P, where the totaling and per capita computations take place.

Text and Formula Entry (See figure 13, Formula Worksheet)

Columns A and B; Width = 12, Text Left
As you did in ACTIVMO, take a copy of ACTIVDAY and delete all the columns but A and B, or LOAD only columns A and B from ACTIVDAY.
Columns C through N; Width = 12, Text Right
Enter the column headings in rows 8 and 9.
Transfer the total activity column to its appropriate place each month.
Column O; Width = 12, Text Right
Enter the SUM formula in O12. REPLICATE it to O13 through O36.
Column P; Width = 12, Text Right
First, enter the text "Enter Jurisdiction Population in Cell G6" in cells F5 and G5. Then enter, as a value, your population in cell G6.
Enter the division formula in cell P12 and REPLICATE it to P13 through P30. You may decide that you do not want to know the per capita ratio for a number of these items. You may delete those that make no sense to you.

Clean up the spreadsheet by erasing the formulas in columns O and P that you do not need.

The previous spreadsheets in the ACTIV series have used public library examples. ACTIVCL is designed as a detailed college library monthly activity report. The detailed categories may be compressed or expanded to meet your needs (figure 14).

It is conceivable that a daily entry form could be designed much like ACTIVDAY. You are welcome to try to design such a spreadsheet, but be forewarned that it will be huge. If you wish to construct a daily entry form, it is probably wise to break ACTIVCL down into smaller spreadsheets.

ACTIVCL: A College Library Monthly Activity Report

General Design Features

There are no especially difficult formulas in this spreadsheet. Entering the text will take the most time. The activity for the month is entered in columns E and L. The data for columns D and K are transferred from the previous month's spreadsheet, columns F and M.

Text and Formula Entry (See figure 15, Formula Worksheet)

Columns A, B, C, and H, I, J; Width = 15, Text Left
Enter the text in the cells indicated.
Columns D, E, F, and K, L, M; Width = 15, Text Right

```
   A   ::   B   ::   C   ::   D   ::   E   ::   F   ::   G   ::   H   ::   I   ::   J   ::   K   ::   L   ::   M   ::   N   ::   O   ::   P
```

 1 : Filename: ACTIVYR
 2 : Date Created:
 3 : Date Last Changed:
 4 : ==
 5 : YEARLY LIBRARY ACTIVITY SUMMARY REPORT
 6 : YEAR OF: Enter Jurisdiction Population In Cell G6   12,000
 7 :

8 : STATISTICAL 9 : CATEGORIES	JAN TOTAL	FEB TOTAL	MAR TOTAL	APR TOTAL	MAY TOTAL	JUNE TOTAL	JULY TOTAL	AUG TOTAL	SEPT TOTAL	OCT TOTAL	NOV TOTAL	DEC TOTAL	1984 TOTAL	PER CAPITA TOTAL
11 : CIRCULATION ACTIVITY:														
12 : Non-Fiction	2800	2900	3000	2800	2900	3000	2800	2900	3000	2800	2900	3000	SUM(C12:N12)	012/G6
13 : Fict on	1700	1800	1900	1700	1800	1900	1700	1800	1900	1700	1800	1900	SUM(C13:N13)	013/G6
14 : Other Material:														
15 : Cassettes	5	10	15	5	10	15	5	10	15	5	10	15	SUM(C15:N15)	015/G6
16 : Posters	10	15	20	10	15	20	10	15	20	10	15	20	SUM(C16:N16)	016/G6
17 : Magazines	500	600	700	500	600	700	500	600	700	500	600	700	SUM(C17:N17)	017/G6
18 : Paperbacks	1000	1100	1200	1000	1100	1200	1000	1100	1200	1000	1100	1200	SUM(C18:N18)	018/G6
19 : Films	40	50	60	40	50	60	40	50	60	40	50	60	SUM(C19:N19)	019/G6
20 : Records	200	300	400	200	300	400	200	300	400	200	300	400	SUM(C20:N20)	020/G6
21 : Other	0	10	20	0	10	20	0	10	20	0	10	20	SUM(C21:N21)	021/G6
22 :														
23 : Subtotal: Other	1755	2085	2415	1755	2085	2415	1755	2085	2415	1755	2085	2415	SUM(C23:N23)	023/G6
24 :														
25 : Total Circulation	6255	6785	7315	6255	6785	7315	6255	6785	7315	6255	6785	7315	SUM(017:023)	025/G6
26 :														
27 : INFORMATION ACTIVITY:														
28 : Reference Questio	1800	1900	2000	1800	1900	2000	1800	1900	2000	1800	1900	2000	SUM(C28:N28)	028/G6
29 : Directional Quest	3500	3600	3700	3500	3600	3700	3500	3600	3700	3500	3600	3700	SUM(C29:N29)	029/G6
30 : Attendance	5000	5500	6000	5000	5500	6000	5000	5500	6000	5000	5500	6000	SUM(C30:N30)	030/G6
31 : Programs Held	20	30	40	20	30	40	20	30	40	20	30	40	SUM(C31:N31)	
32 : Program Attendanc	500	550	600	500	550	600	500	550	600	500	550	600	SUM(C32:N32)	
33 : Borrowers Registe	25	30	35	25	30	35	25	30	35	25	30	35	SUM(C33:N33)	
34 : Borrowers Withdra	10	15	20	10	15	20	10	15	20	10	15	20	SUM(C34:N34)	
35 : Hours Open	250	300	350	250	300	350	250	300	350	250	300	350	SUM(C35:N35)	
36 : Days Open	25	25	25	25	25	25	25	25	25	25	25	25	SUM(C36:N36)	

Figure 13.   ACTIVYR: Yearly Library Activity Summary Report, Formula Worksheet

	A	B	C	D	E	F	G	H	I	J	K	L	M
1	Filename:		ACTIVCL										
2	Date Created:												
3	Date Last Changed:												
4	====												
5	COLLEGE LIBRARY MONTHLY ACTIVITY REPORT												
6	MONTH OF:	September											
7													

Left section

Label	Y-T-D PRIOR MONTH	ACTIVITY THIS MONTH	Y-T-D THIS MONTH
ACQUISITIONS			
Monograph vols added	2,000	1,000	3,000
Periodical vols added	800	50	850
Total vols added	2,800	1,050	3,850
Vols withdrawn	600	100	700
Net vols added	2,200	950	3,150
U.S. docs added (print)	3,000	200	3,200
U.S. docs added (fiche)	30,000	500	30,500
State docs added	600	50	650
U.N. Docs added (print)	400	100	500
U.N. Docs added (fiche)	500	400	900
PERIODICALS			
New subscriptions	20	10	30
Discontinued subscr.	5	5	10
Net subscr. added	25	5	30
Vols added by binding	500	10	510
Titles added (m/film)	60	150	210
Titles added (fiche)	50	50	100
BINDING AND REPAIR			
Vols sent (bindery)	500	150	650
Vols received (bindery)	450	120	570
Vols sent (repair)	125	50	175
Vols received (repair)	100	30	130
MICROFORMS ADDED			
Microfilm reels	400	150	550
Microfiche pieces	5,000	2,500	7,500
CATALOGING			
Titles cataloged			
Print	1,200	500	1,700
M/film	50	25	75
M/fiche	100	50	150
Volumes cataloged			
Print	1,500	800	2,300
M/film	100	30	130
M/fiche	200	60	260
Total volumes cataloged	1,800	890	2,690

Right section

Label	Y-T-D PRIOR MONTH	ACTIVITY THIS MONTH	Y-T-D THIS MONTH
CATALOGING (cont'd)			
Volumes re-cataloged	500	75	575
Catalog cards filed	5,000	1,000	6,000
Catalog cards produced			
OCLC	4,000	500	4,500
Other	150	25	175
Total	4,150	525	4,675
Catalog cards corrected	200	150	350
Phonodiscs cataloged	150	15	165
Audio-cassettes cat'd	50	5	55
Video-cassettes cat'd	25	1	26
CIRCULATION			
General circulation	8,500	3,000	11,500
Phono records	250	50	300
Pamphlets	100	5	105
Overnight reserves:			
Books	3,000	1,000	4,000
Tapes & records	500	20	520
Total circulation	12,350	4,075	16,425
INTERLIBRARY LOAN			
Items borrowed	500	100	600
Items loaned	650	150	800
REFERENCE			
On-line searches	600	50	650
Reference questions	5,500	1,500	7,000

HOLDINGS SUMMARY	HOLDINGS THRU LAST MONTH	HOLDINGS THRU THIS MONTH
Monograph/Periodical vols	390,000	390,950
Documents	220,000	221,250
Microfilm	20,000	20,150
Microfiche	65,000	67,500
Periodical subscrs	1,500	1,505

Figure 14. ACTIVCL: College Library Monthly Activity Report, Example Spreadsheet

	A	B	C	D	E	F	G	H	I	J	K	L	M
1	Filename:												
2	Date Created:												
3	Date Last Changed:												
4	=========		ACTIVCL										
5	COLLEGE LIBRARY MONTHLY ACTIVITY REPORT												
6	MONTH OF: September												
7													
8				Y-T-D PRIOR MONTH	ACTIVITY THIS MONTH	Y-T-D THIS MONTH					Y-T-D PRIOR MONTH	ACTIVITY THIS MONTH	Y-T-D THIS MONTH
9													
10													
11	ACQUISITIONS							CATALOGING (cont'd)					
12		Monograph vols added		2000	1000	D12+E12			Volumes re-cataloged		500	75	K12+L12
13		Periodical vols added		800	50	D13+E13			Catalog cards filed		5000	1000	K13+L13
14		Total vols added		2800	E12+E13	D14+E14			Catalog cards produced				K14+L14
15		Vols withdrawn		600	100	D15+E15			OCLC		4000	500	K15+L15
16		Net vols added		2200	E14-E15	D16+E16			Other		150	25	K16+L16
17									Total		4150	L15+L16	L17+L17
18		U.S. docs added (print)		3000	200	D18+E18			Catalog cards corrected		200	150	K18+L18
19		U.S. docs added (fiche)		30000	500	D19+E19							
20		State docs added		600	50	D20+E20			Phonodiscs cataloged		150	15	K20+L20
21		U.N. Docs added (print)		400	100	D21+E21			Audio-cassettes cat'd		50	5	K21+L21
22		U.N. Docs added (fiche)		500	400	D22+E22			Video-cassettes cat'd		25	1	K22+L22
23													
24	PERIODICALS							CIRCULATION					
25		New subscriptions		20	10	D25+E25			General circulation		8500	3000	K25+L25
26		Discontinued subscr.		5	5	D26+E26			Phono records		250	50	K26+L26
27		Net subscr. added		25	E25-E26	D27+E27			Pamphlets		100	5	K27+L27
28									Overnight reserves:				
29		Vols added by binding		500	10	D29+E29			Books		3000	1000	K29+L29
30		Titles added (m/film)		60	150	D30+E30			Tapes & records		500	20	K30+L30
31		Titles added (fiche)		50	50	D31+E31			Total circulation		12350	SUM(L25:L27,L29:L30)	K31+L31
32													
33	BINDING AND REPAIR							INTERLIBRARY LOAN					
34		Vols sent (bindery)		500	150	D34+E34			Items borrowed		500	100	K34+L34
35		Vols received (bindery)		450	120	D35+E35			Items loaned		650	150	K35+L35
36		Vols sent (repair)		125	50	D36+E36							
37		Vols received (repair)		100	30	D37+E37							
38								REFERENCE					
39	MICROFORMS ADDED								On-line searches		600	50	K38+L38
40		Microfilm reels		400	150	D40+E40			Reference questions		5500	1500	K39+L39
41		Microfiche pieces		5000	2500	D41+E41							
42											HOLDINGS THRU LAST MONTH	HOLDINGS THRU THIS MONTH	
43	CATALOGING							HOLDINGS SUMMARY					
44		Titles cataloged											
45		Print		1200	500	D45+E45			Monograph/Periodical vols		390000	E16+K45	
46		M/film		50	25	D46+E46			Documents		220000	SUM(E18:E22)+K46	
47		M/fiche		100	50	D47+E47			Microfilm		20000	E40+K47	
48		Volumes cataloged							Microfiche		65000	E41+K48	
49		Print		1500	800	D49+E49			Periodical subscrs		1500	E27+K49	
50		M/film		100	30	D50+E50							
51		M/fiche		200	60	D51+E51							
52		Total volumes cataloged		1800	E49+E50+E51	D52+E52							

Figure 15.   ACTIVCL: College Library Monthly Activity Report, Formula Worksheet

Column D

All the data will be transferred from the previous month's report.

Column E

Enter the formulas in the appropriate cells.

Column F

Enter the first formula in cell F12 and REPLICATE it to F13 through F52.

Column G

This column is left blank.

Column K

The data in cells K12 through K39 are transferred from the previous month's report.

The first time you use the spreadsheet, enter your inventoried holdings in cells K44 through K49. Thereafter, transfer the previous month's holdings total to this position.

Column L

Enter the formulas in their appropriate cells.

Column M

Enter the first formula in M12 and REPLICATE it to M13 through M39.

Clean up the spreadsheet by erasing any unwanted formulas in columns F and M where you have replicated continuously.

Statistics on additions and withdrawals of items from the collection are commonly maintained in libraries. COLLECT assembles those statistics, using a public library as an example.

In addition to the activity that occurs for each of the various reporting categories, the COLLECT spreadsheet also maintains a current balance of items in the collection (figure 16). Thus the spreadsheet that represents the last month in the reporting year will contain information that is commonly requested by outside reporting agencies, such as number of nonfiction, fiction, and AV materials held at year's end.

COLLECT: A Monthly Summary of Collection Activity

General Design Features

The two columns C and D represent the balance on hand at the conclusion of the previous month. When you first construct the spreadsheet you will have to enter the balance on hand as of that point. Thereafter, you can update each month's spreadsheet by transferring the balances in columns I and J to columns C and D in the same manner as was suggested in the discussion of the EXPEND spreadsheet ("Using the Model").

Overall, the spreadsheet contains no difficult formulas or formating problems.

Text and Formula Entry (See figure 17, Formula Worksheet)

Columns A and B; Width = 12, Text Left

Enter all the text into column A, with column B as a spillover column. You can indent text, as illustrated, by entering several spaces before you actually type the text entry.

The long lines in rows 4, 7, 10, and 44 can be drawn by using the REPEAT ENTRY function.

Figure 16. COLLECT:
Monthly Summary of
Collection Activity,
Example Spreadsheet

	A	B	C	D	E	F	G	H	I	J
1	Filename:		COLLECT							
2	Date Created:									
3	Date Last Changed:									
4	==									
5	MONTHLY COLLECTION ACTIVITY									
6	MONTH OF: March									
7	– –									
8	Item		Titles	Volumes	Titles	Volumes	Titles	Volumes	Balance	Balance
9	Description		On Hand	On Hand	Added	Added	W/drawn	W/drawn	Titles	Volumes
10	....									
11	Dewey Class									
12	000		2,500	2,700	200	210	10	10	2,690	2,900
13	100		3,000	3,500	250	260	12	14	3,238	3,746
14	200		5,000	5,500	400	400	14	16	5,386	5,884
15	300		8,000	8,500	650	660	16	18	8,634	9,142
16	400		1,000	1,100	80	100	0	0	1,080	1,200
17	500		7,000	7,500	550	575	20	22	7,530	8,053
18	600		10,000	12,000	800	825	22	24	10,778	12,801
19	700		11,000	13,000	900	925	24	26	11,876	13,899
20	800		6,000	6,500	500	525	26	28	6,474	6,997
21	900		5,000	5,500	400	425	18	20	5,382	5,905
22			----	----	----	----	----	----	----	----
23	Total Dewey		58,500	65,800	4,730	4,905	162	178	63,068	70,527
24	Fiction								0	0
25	Mysteries		3,000	3,100	250	250	0	0	3,250	3,350
26	Sci Fi		1,500	1,500	125	125	0	0	1,625	1,625
27	Romance		2,500	2,500	200	200	5	5	2,695	2,695
28	Westerns		1,000	1,000	80	80	0	0	1,080	1,080
29	Other		500	500	40	40	0	0	540	540
30			----	----	----	----	----	----	----	----
31	Total Fiction		8,000	8,100	655	655	5	5	8,650	8,750
32	Paperbacks		5,000	5,100	400	400	10	10	5,390	5,490
33	Government Docs		10,000	12,000	800	850	0	0	10,800	12,850
34	Periodicals		800	4,000	60	100	0	0	860	4,100
35	Large Print		500	500	40	40	0	0	540	540
36	Audiovisual Material								0	0
37	Disc Recordings		2,500	2,500	200	200	1	1	2,699	2,699
38	Cassettes		1,000	1,000	80	80	5	2	1,075	1,078
39	Videotapes/discs		500	500	40	40	0	0	540	540
40	Films		100	100	10	10	0	0	110	110
41	Other		50	50	5	5	0	0	55	55
42			----	----	----	----	----	----	----	----
43	Total A-V Material		4,150	4,150	335	335	6	3	4,479	4,482
44	....									
45	Grand Total		86,950	99,650	7,020	7,285	183	196	93,787	106,739

Columns C through H; Width = 12, Text Right

Enter the column headings in rows 8 and 9.

Enter the four SUM formulas in column C. At the same time, enter the underscored lines in rows 22, 30, and 42.

REPLICATE each of the formulas and the underscored lines to columns D through H.

Columns I and J; Width = 12, Text Right

Enter the column headings in rows 8 and 9.

Enter the formula (C12+E13)−G12 in cell I12.

REPLICATE the formula in I12 to I13 through I45.

Enter the formula (D12+F12)−H12 in cell J12.

REPLICATE the formula in J12 to J13 through J45.

BLANK or ERASE the entries in rows 22, 30, 42, and 44 for columns I and J. Replace these entries with underscored lines.

COLLECT

	A	B	C	D	E	F	G	H	I	J
1	Filename:									
2	Date Created:									
3	Date Last Changed:									
4	===									
5	MONTHLY COLLECTION ACTIVITY									
6	MONTH OF:		March							
7										
8	Item		Titles	Volumes	Titles	Volumes	Titles	Volumes	Balance	Balance
9	Description		On Hand	On Hand	Added	Added	W/drawn	W/drawn	Titles	Volumes
10										
11	Dewey Class									
12	000		2500	2700	200	210	10	10	(C12+E12)-G12	(D12+F12)-H12
13	100		3000	3500	250	260	12	14	(C13+E13)-G13	(D13+F13)-H13
14	200		5000	5500	400	400	14	16	(C14+E14)-G14	(D14+F14)-H14
15	300		8000	8500	650	660	16	18	(C15+E15)-G15	(D15+F15)-H15
16	400		1000	1100	80	100	0	0	(C16+E16)-G16	(D16+F16)-H16
17	500		7000	7500	550	575	20	22	(C17+E17)-G17	(D17+F17)-H17
18	600		10000	12000	800	825	22	24	(C18+E18)-G18	(D18+F18)-H18
19	700		11000	13000	900	925	24	26	(C19+E19)-G19	(D19+F19)-H19
20	800		6000	6500	500	525	26	28	(C20+E20)-G20	(D20+F20)-H20
21	900		5000	5500	400	425	18	20	(C21+E21)-G21	(D21+F21)-H21
22										
23	Total Dewey		SUM(C12:C21)	SUM(D12:D21)	SUM(E12:E21)	SUM(F12:F21)	SUM(G12:G21)	SUM(H12:H21)	(C23+E23)-G23	(D23+F23)-H23
24	Fiction									
25	Mysteries		3000	3100	250	250	0	0	(C25+E25)-G25	(D25+F25)-H25
26	Sci Fi		1500	1500	125	125	0	0	(C26+E26)-G26	(D26+F26)-H26
27	Romance		2500	2500	200	200	5	5	(C27+E27)-G27	(D27+F27)-H27
28	Westerns		1000	1000	80	80	0	0	(C28+E28)-G28	(D28+F28)-H28
29	Other		500	500	40	40	0	0	(C29+E29)-G29	(D29+F29)-H29
30										
31	Total Fiction		SUM(C25:C28)	SUM(D25:D28)	SUM(E25:E28)	SUM(F25:F28)	SUM(G25:G28)	SUM(H25:H28)	(C31+E31)-G31	(D31+F31)-H31
32	Paperbacks		5000	5100	400	400	10	10	(C32+E32)-G32	(D32+F32)-H32
33	Government Docs		10000	12000	800	850	0	0	(C33+E33)-G33	(D33+F33)-H33
34	Periodicals		800	4000	60	100	0	0	(C34+E34)-G34	(D34+F34)-H34
35	Large Print		500	500	40	40	0	0	(C35+E35)-G35	(D35+F35)-H35
36	Audiovisual Material									
37	Disc Recordings		2500	2500	200	200	1	1	(C37+E37)-G37	(D37+F37)-H37
38	Cassettes		1000	1000	80	80	5	2	(C38+E38)-G38	(D38+F38)-H38
39	Videotapes/discs		500	500	40	40	0	0	(C39+E39)-G39	(D39+F39)-H39
40	Films		100	100	10	10	0	0	(C40+E40)-G40	(D40+F40)-H40
41	Other		50	50	5	5	0	0	(C41+E41)-G41	(D41+F41)-H41
42										
43	Total A-V Material		SUM(C37:C41)	SUM(D37:D41)	SUM(E37:E41)	SUM(F37:F41)	SUM(G37:G41)	SUM(H37:H41)	(C43+E43)-G43	(D43+F43)-H43
44										
45	Grand Total		SUM(C23,C31:C35,C43)	SUM(D23,D31:D35,D43)	SUM(E23,E31:E35,E43)	SUM(F23,F31:F35,F43)	SUM(G23,G31:G35,G43)	SUM(H23,H31:H35,H43)	(C45+E45)-G45	(D45+F45)-H45

Figure 17. COLLECT: Monthly Summary of Collection Activity, Formula Worksheet

Using the Model

Each month, enter the titles and volumes added and withdrawn in columns E through H. Update the "Titles" and "Volumes on Hand" figures in columns C and D by transferring the contents of the previous month's balances (columns I and J) to this location. Remember to transfer just the values and not the formulas.

Obviously, this model will have to be modified if your reporting categories are different from the example. Academic libraries will have to make the most sizable changes in the spreadsheet. However, the simplicity of the summation formulas should make this an easy task.

PAY: A Payroll Distribution Record

The idea for this spreadsheet came as a request from Elaine McConnell when she was director of the Piscataway Public Library in New Jersey. (She is now director of the Ocean County (N.J.) Library.) Elaine needed some method of determining the number of hours worked and the costs of personnel across her three facilities. Many of her staff were assigned to more than one facility, but no recordkeeping system was in operation to account for multiple work sites for her staff.

PAY (figure 18) uses a variety of the functions of spreadsheet programs, including LOOKUP and IF statements (see figure 19). This is one of the more exotic spreadsheets in this book and should be studied closely. The techniques used here have broad applicability.

General Design Features

Once PAY is constructed, the hours worked by each individual at each location for the pay period are entered in columns E, F, and G. The spreadsheet program then takes over and calculates the proper hourly rate, allocates the total dollars to each location, and sums the hours worked and wages paid columns. The totals for the pay period are then transferred to the bottom of the spreadsheet, where they are accumulated, and a year-to-date total is computed.

Two different pay schedules are allowed in this spreadsheet: salaried staff and hourly staff. For salaried staff, the annual salary is entered in column B and the hourly rate is computed, based on a 35-hour work week. (The formula can be changed to reflect different lengths of work weeks.) For hourly staff, each person is assigned an hourly classification (column C), which is then looked up in the LOOKUP table contained in columns M and N. Thus if a person is in hourly class 9, the hourly rate is $10 per hour.

A glance at the PAY formula worksheet (figure 19) reveals a complicated formula in column D. The formula is a combination of an IF statement and the LOOKUP function. Here is what the formula in cell D12 means. The formula is

$$IF(B12>0,B12/1820,LOOKUP(C12,M12:M20))$$

That is, IF the salary in cell B12 is greater than zero, divide that salary in B12 by 1820, which is the number of hours in a work year for a 35-hour work week, and place the results in cell D12. But IF the salary in B12 is zero, LOOKUP the number in the hourly classification column (column C), in the table in column M, and place the value that is next to it in column N in this cell (i.e., cell D12).

	A	B	C	D	E	F	G	H	I	J	K	L	M	N
1	Filename:	PAY												
2	Date Created:													
3	Date Last Changed:													
4	===													
5	PAYROLL DISTRIBUTION RECORD													
6	Payroll Period: From ———— To ————													
7														
8	Name	Annual	Hourly	Hrly Rate	Hrs Wkd	Hrs Wkd	Hrs Wkd	Total	Alloc	Alloc	Alloc	Wages	Ref.	Wage
9		Salary	Classif.		Main	Branch	Bkmb	Hrs. Wkd	Main	Branch	Bkmb	Paid		Rate
10														
11	PROFESSIONAL STAFF													
12	Smith	$30,000.00		$16.48	35	0		35	$576.92			$576.92	1	$3.50
13	Jones	$24,000.00		$13.19	7	28		35	$92.31	$369.23		$461.54	2	$4.00
14	Adams	$22,000.00		$12.09	35			35	$423.08			$423.08	3	$4.50
15	O'Shaw		9	$10.00	12	7		19	$120.00	$70.00		$190.00	4	$5.00
16													5	$6.00
17	NON-PROFESSIONAL STAFF												6	$7.00
18	Roberts	$18,000.00		$9.89	35			35	$346.15			$346.15	7	$8.00
19	Paul	$15,000.00		$8.24		35		35		$288.46		$288.46	8	$9.00
20	Joyce	$15,000.00		$8.24	21	14		35	$173.08	$115.38		$288.46	9	$10.00
21	Clark		1	$3.50			15	15			$52.50	$52.50		
22	James		4	$5.00	0	7	7	14		$35.00	$35.00	$70.00		
23														
24	Totals				145	91	22	258	$1,731.54	$878.08	$87.50	$2,697.12		
25														
26	CUMULATIVE YEAR TO DATE SUMMARY													
27	Pay Period	Frcm:		To:	Hrs Wkd Main	Hrs Wkd Branch	Hrs Wkd Bkmb	Total Hrs. Wkd	Alloc Main	Alloc Branch	Alloc Bkmb	Wages Paid		
28														
29	1				140	102	25	267	$1,566.15	$1,068.46	$98.00	$2,732.62		
30	2				126	120	22	268	$1,496.15	$1,178.46	$87.50	$2,762.12		
31	3				138	105	22	265	$1,616.15	$1,063.46	$87.50	$2,767.12		
32	4				145	91	22	258	$1,731.54	$878.08	$87.50	$2,697.12		
33	5													
34	6													
35														
36	Year to Date Total				549	418	91	1,058	$6,410.00	$4,188.46	$360.50	$10,958.96		

Figure 18. PAY: Payroll Distribution Record, Example Spreadsheet

Text and Formula Entry (See figure 19, Formula Worksheet)

Column A; Width = 12, Text Left

Enter the text in the suggested cells. Two major categories of staff are given here: professional and nonprofessional staff.

Enter the long lines, using the REPEAT ENTRY function.

Columns B through N; Width = 12, Text Right

Enter the column headings in rows 8 and 9.

Column B

Enter the annual salary for each employee. If an employee is part time or on an hourly pay schedule, enter nothing or zero.

Column C

Enter the classification number for hourly employees. This class number must match an hourly figure in column N.

Column D

Enter the formula in cell D12. REPLICATE the formula from cells D12 to D13 through D22.

Column E

Enter several dashes in cell E23. REPLICATE the entry to cells F23 through L23.

Enter the SUM formula in cell E24. REPLICATE the formula in E24 to F24 through L24.

Enter the SUM formula in cell E36. REPLICATE the formula in E36 to F36 through L36.

COPY or REPLICATE the column headings for columns E through L in rows 8 and 9 to rows 26 and 27.

Columns F and G

Except for the entry of the hours worked data, all formulas and headings should be already there because of what you did in column E above.

Column H

SUM the hours worked columns, using the formula given in cell H12. REPLICATE cells H12 to H13 through H22.

Column I

MULTIPLY the hourly rate in cell D12 by the hours worked in the main library (cell E12). REPLICATE cells I12 to I13 through I22.

Column J

MULTIPLY the hourly rate in cell D12 by the hours worked in the branch library (cell F12). REPLICATE cells J12 to J13 through J22.

Column K

MULTIPLY the hourly rate in cell D12 by the hours worked on the bookmobile (cell G12). REPLICATE cells K12 to K13 through K22.

Column L

SUM the wages paid by adding cells I12, J12, and K12 in cell L12. REPLICATE cell L12 to L13 through L22.

Column M

Enter the hourly classification codes in column M. They must be in ascending order if LOOKUP is to work properly.

Column N

Enter the hourly rate that corresponds to the code given in column M.

Clean up the spreadsheet by erasing or blanking the formulas that are in rows 16 and 17.

	A	B	C	D	E	F	G	H	I	J	K	L	M	N
1	Filename:		PAY											
2	Date Created:													
3	Date Last Changed:													
4	======													
5	PAYROLL DISTRIBUTION RECORD													
6	Payroll Period: From ——————— To ———————													
7	---													
8	Name	Annual Salary	Hourly Classif.	Hrly Rate	Hrs Wkd Main	Hrs Wkd Branch	Hrs Wkd Bkmb	Total Hrs. Wkd	Alloc Main	Alloc Branch	Alloc Bkmb	Wages Paid	Ref.	Wage Rate
11	PROFESSIONAL STAFF													
12	Smith	30000		IF(B12>0,B12/1820,LOOKUP(C12,M12:M20))	35	0		E12+F12+G12	D12*E12	D12*F12	D12*G12	I12+J12+K12	1	3.50
13	Jones	24000		IF(B13>0,B13/1820,LOOKUP(C13,M12:M20))	7	28		E13+F13+G13	D13*E13	D13*F13	D13*G13	I13+J13+K13	2	4
14	Adams	22000		IF(B14>0,B14/1820,LOOKUP(C14,M12:M20))	35			E14+F14+G14	D14*E14	D14*F14	D14*G14	I14+J14+K14	3	4.5
15	O'Shaw		9	IF(B15>0,B15/1820,LOOKUP(C15,M12:M20))	12	7		E15+F15+G15	D15*E15	D15*F15	D15*G15	I15+J15+K15	4	5
16													5	6
17	NON-PROFESSIONAL STAFF												6	7
18	Roberts	18000		IF(B18>0,B18/1820,LOOKUP(C18,M12:M20))	35			E18+F18+G18	D18*E18	D18*F18	D18*G18	I18+J18+K18	7	8
19	Paul	15000		IF(B19>0,B19/1820,LOOKUP(C19,M12:M20))		35		E19+F19+G19	D19*E19	D19*F19	D19*G19	I19+J19+K19	8	9
20	Joyce	15000		IF(B20>0,B20/1820,LOOKUP(C20,M12:M20))	21	14		E20+F20+G20	D20*E20	D20*F20	D20*G20	I20+J20+K20	9	10
21	Clark		1	IF(B21>0,B21/1820,LOOKUP(C21,M12:M20))			15	E21+F21+G21	D21*E21	D21*F21	D21*G21	I21+J21+K21		
22	James		4	IF(B22>0,B22/1820,LOOKUP(C22,M12:M20))	0	7	7	E22+F22+G22	D22*E22	D22*F22	D22*G22	I22+J22+K22		
23	---													
24	Totals				SUM(E12:E22)	SUM(F12:F22)	SUM(G12:G22)	SUM(H12:H22)	SUM(I12:I22)	SUM(J12:J22)	SUM(K12:K22)	SUM(L12:L22)		
25	---													
26	CUMULATIVE YEAR TO DATE SUMMARY													
27	Pay Period	From:		To:	Hrs Wkd Main	Hrs Wkd Branch	Hrs Wkd Bkmb	Total Hrs. Wkd	Alloc Main	Alloc Branch	Alloc Bkmb	Wages Paid		
28	...													
29	1													
30	2													
31	3													
32	4													
33	5													
34	6													
35	...													
36	Year to Date Total				SUM(E29:E34)	SUM(F29:F34)	SUM(G29:G34)	SUM(H29:H34)	SUM(I29:I34)	SUM(J29:J34)	SUM(K29:K34)	SUM(L29:L34)		

Figure 19. PAY: Payroll Distribution Record, Formula Worksheet

Using the Model

At the end of each pay period, enter the hours worked by each individual in the column associated with a location. After you have entered all the hours worked, use the COPY or REPLICATE command to transfer the values (not the formulas) in row 24 to one of the rows at the bottom of the spreadsheet, starting with row 29. For example, the first pay period of the fiscal year would go into row 29, the second into row 30, and so on. You must extend the spreadsheet beyond row 34 in order to enter all the pay periods for a year (most likely 26 in all).

Several modifications of the PAY spreadsheet may be desirable. The first would be to include a column for vacation hours so that the total-wages-paid summary would cross-check with other payroll summaries. The second is more difficult. That is, how to account for overtime pay when the additional hours worked are at a different rate than regular time? One solution is to insert three more columns for the hours worked, which would be used to enter the number of overtime hours. The allocation columns would then have to pick up the regular hours times the regular rate plus the overtime hours times the overtime rate, which would be contained on a second LOOKUP table. (I'm sure some enterprising spreadsheet hacker can work out this solution.)

CJFORM: A Model to Calculate the Clapp-Jordan Formula for College and University Libraries

The Clapp-Jordan Formula[1] in spreadsheet form is an excellent illustration of the "What if?" capability of spreadsheet programs (figure 20). Here, for example, we might ask: "What if the university added two new master's programs and one Ph.D. program? What changes in the collection would be required, based on the Clapp-Jordan Formula?"

Clapp and Jordan set out to estimate the number of book, periodical, and document titles and volumes needed to support an academic curriculum. They established a base level for an undergraduate library and then added specific numbers of titles and volumes based on six local factors: number of faculty members, number of FTE students, number of undergraduates in honors or independent study programs, number of undergraduate major fields, number of master's fields, and number of doctoral fields.

Based on these factors, a college or university can determine where it falls behind or exceeds the recommended amounts. Using the spreadsheet, a college or university can estimate what additions would be required as it increases any one or a combination of the factors.

General Design Features

The CJFORM formula worksheet (figure 21) multiplies the local college-size figures by the formula amount provided by Clapp and Jordan. It sums each factor to give a total volume count needed, based on each factor, and also sums the types of materials needed. By entering your current holdings of books, periodicals, and documents you can determine where you fall short (or exceed) the Clapp-Jordan recommendations.

Text and Formula Entry (See figure 21, Formula Worksheet)

Columns A through B; Width = 12, Text Left
Enter the text and long lines in the rows indicated. You may indent the indicated text by inserting several leading blanks.
Columns C through J; Width = 12, Text Right

1. Verner W. Clapp and Robert T. Jordan, "Quantitative Criteria for Adequacy of Academic Library Collections," *College and Research Libraries*, 26:371–80 (1965).

	A	B	C	D	E	F	G	H	I	J	
1	Filename:		CJFORM								
2	Date Created:										
3	Date Last Changed:										
4	==
5	CLAPP-JORDAN FORMULA
6	– –
7				DATA		BOOKS			PERIODICALS		DOCUMENTS	TOTAL
8				ENTRY	Titles	Volumes		Titles	Volumes	Volumes	Volumes
9	....
10	MINIMUM REQUIREMENT
11	1. Undergraduate Library				35,000	42,000		250	3,750	5,000	50,750
12	ADDITIONS
13	2. Faculty Members (FTE)			650	32,500	39,000		650	9,750	16,250	65,000
14	3. Students (FTE)			18,000		180,000			18,000	18,000	216,000
15	4. Undergraduate Honors Students			578	5,780	6,936					6,936
16	5. Undergraduate Major Fields			56	11,200	13,440		168	2,520	2,800	18,760
17	6. Master's Fields			24	48,000	57,600		240	3,600	12,000	73,200
18	7. Doctoral Fields			16	240,000	288,000		1,600	24,000	80,000	392,000
19					————	————		————	————	————	————
20	Computed Requirements				372,480	626,976		2,908	61,620	134,050	822,646
21	Present Holdings				450,000	600,000		3,000	62,000	150,000	812,000
22	Difference: Held minus Computed				77,520	-26,976		92	380	15,950	-10,646

Figure 20. CJFORM: Model to Calculate the Clapp-Jordan Formula, Example Spreadsheet

Column D

This column is reserved for your data entry.

Column E

Enter the numbers and formulas as given on the formula worksheet.
REPLICATE the SUM formula in cell E20 to F20 through I20.
REPLICATE the subtraction formula in cell E22 to F22 through I22.

Columns F through I

Enter the numbers and formulas as given on the formula worksheet.

Column J

Enter the number in cell J11.
Enter the addition formula in cell J13. REPLICATE cell J13 to J14 through J22.
Return to column E and enter the series of dashes in cell E19.
REPLICATE cells E19 to F19 through J19.

Make sure that the following cells are empty: E14, G14, G15, H15, and I15. If you have stray numbers or formulas in these cells, the addition will be incorrect.

VOIGT: A Model to Calculate Acquisition Rates in University Libraries

Melvin J. Voigt's method of determining the yearly acquisition rates for university libraries is similar to the Clapp-Jordan approach in that it is formula driven.[2] That is, a certain number of materials must be purchased each year to support various areas of the university curriculum. However, Voigt deals with yearly acquisitions of material while Clapp and Jordan deal with total holdings in the collection.

Voigt starts with a base number of items that are to be added yearly. He then subtracts from this figure certain amounts of new acquisitions if there are not a certain number of Ph.D. programs in certain areas. He then recommends additional new acquisitions for advanced graduate and professional programs, numbers of undergraduate students, the amount of money received for sponsored research, and additional ac-

2. Melvin J. Voigt, "Acquisition Rates in University Libraries," *College and Research Libraries*, 36(4): 263–71 (1975).

	A	B	C	D	E	F	G	H	I	J
									DOCUMENTS	TOTAL
				DATA	BOOKS		PERIODICALS		Volumes	Volumes
				ENTRY	Titles	Volumes	Titles	Volumes		
1	Filename:		CJFORM							
2	Date Created:									
3	Date Last Changed:									
4	=========									
5	CLAPP-JORDAN FORMULA									
6	---------									
7				DATA	BOOKS		PERIODICALS		DOCUMENTS	TOTAL
8				ENTRY	Titles	Volumes	Titles	Volumes	Volumes	Volumes
9										
10	MINIMUM REQUIREMENT									
11	1. Undergraduate Library				35000	42000	250	3750	5000	50750
12	ADDITIONS									
13	2. Faculty Members (FTE)			650	D13*50	D13*60	D13*1	D13*15	D13*25	F13+H13+I13
14	3. Students (FTE)			1800		D14*10		D14*1	D14*1	F14+H14+I14
15	4. Undergraduate Honors Students			578	D15*10	D15*12				F15+H15+I15
16	5. Undergraduate Major Fields			56	D16*200	D16*240	D16*3	D16*45	D16*50	F16+H16+I16
17	6. Master's Fields			24	D17*2000	D17*2400	D17*10	D17*150	D17*500	F17+H17+I17
18	7. Doctoral Fields			16	D18*15000	D18*18000	D18*100	D18*1500	D18*5000	F18+H18+I18
19										
20	Computed Requirements				SUM(E11:E18)	SUM(F11:F18)	SUM(G11:G18)	SUM(H11:H18)	SUM(I11:I18)	F20+H20+I20
21	Present Holdings				450000	600000	3000	62000	150000	F21+H21+I21
22	Difference: Held minus Computed				E21-E20	F21-F20	G21-G20	H21-H20	I21-I20	F22+H22+I22

Figure 21. CJFORM: Model to Calculate the Clapp-Jordan Formula, Formula Worksheet

quisitions if the university is located in less accessible areas (i.e., not close to another major research library).

The model (figure 22) can be used both to establish the current need for acquisitions and to project the impact on the collection of the addition or deletion of various university instructional programs.

General Design Features

The data for your institution are entered in column F and the formulas compute the requirements in column G.

In terms of the design of spreadsheets, this model offers several interesting examples of spreadsheet functions. Looking at figure 23, the formula worksheet, you can see that it includes nested IF statements (i.e., IF statements within IF statements), a combination of IF and AND in the same formula, and two LOOKUP tables. Four of the formulas will be discussed here due to their complexity and uniqueness.

In general, an IF statement is read as follows:

$$IF(A1=5,1000,0)$$

Here, the statement says that IF the value in cell A1 exactly equals 5, place the number 1000 in the current cell. If it does not equal 5, place a zero in the current cell. "Current cell" refers to the position occupied by the formula.

In cell G11 is a lengthy formula which illustrates the use of nested IF statements:

$$IF(F11=2,1000,IF(F11=1,2000,IF(F11=0,3000,0)))$$

This formula is used to reduce the acquisition rate if there are fewer than three social science Ph.D. programs at the university. If there are three or more, no reduction in the overall rate of acquisition is recommended.

For each increment of a program, 1000 items are deducted from the overall total. Thus if there are only two programs, 1000 items are deducted. If there is only one program, 2000 items are deducted; and if there are no programs, 3000 items are deducted.

The formula in cell G11 does this calculation. The actual deduction is performed in cell G56, where the total acquisitions are summed minus the sum of the deducted items, which appears in cell G14.

Cell G13 contains a combination of an IF and an AND statement. The formula in G13 is

$$IF(AND(F12=0,F13=0),1000,0)$$

This formula tests to see if there is neither a Ph.D. program in psychology nor a Ph.D. program in philosophy. If there is neither program, then 1000 items are deducted from the acquisition rate. If there is either one or the other or both, no deduction is made. The formula reads IF there is a zero in F12 AND a zero in F13, place 1000 in cell G13; otherwise, place a zero in cell G13.

The third formula that illustrates how to deal with conditional statements is in cell G29. Again, it is a nested IF statement. The formula reads:

$$IF(F29>3,4000,IF(F29=0,0,F29*1000))$$

Here Voigt is saying that if there are four or more engineering programs, add 4000 items to the acquisition rate. However, if there are fewer than four programs, add only 1000 for each program.

	A	B	C	D	E	F	G	H	I
1	Filename:	VOIGT							
2	Date Created:								
3	Date Last Changed:								
4	==								
5	VOIGT ACQUISITIONS MODEL FOR GENERAL UNIVERSITY LIBRARIES								
6	Melvin J. Voigt, "Acquisition Rates in University Libraries", C&RL, 36(4), 1975, pp. 263-271								
7									
8	M.1: BASE						40,000		
9	M.2: SUBTRACTION								
10	NUMBER OF EUROPEAN LANGUAGE PH.D. PROGRAMS					1	1,000	0	1000
11	NUMBER OF SOCIAL SCIENCE PH.D. PROGRAMS					5	0	1	2000
12	PSYCHOLOGY PH.D. (1=YES, 0=NO)					1		2	3000
13	PHILOSOPHY PH.D. (1=YES, 0=NO)					0	1,000	3	4000
14								4	5000
15	M.3: ADDITION FOR ADVANCED GRADUATE PROGRAMS							5	6000
16	NUMBER OF ADDITIONAL FOREIGN LITERATURE PH.D.'S					2	4,000	6	7000
17	SOCIAL SCIENCE PH.D.'S (SEE ABOVE)					5	10,000	7	8000
18	EARTH SCIENCE PH.D. PROGRAMS					1	2,000		
19	ASTRONOMY PH.D. PROGRAM					0	0	0	0
20								1	1000
21	M.4 ADVANCED GRADUATE AND PROFESSIONAL PROGRAMS							2	2000
22	AGRICULTURE					1	5,000	3	3000
23	ARCHITECTURE					1	1,000	4	4000
24	ART					1	3,000	5	5000
25	BUSINESS ADMINISTRATION					1	2,000	6	6000
26	CITY AND REGIONAL PLANNING					1	0	7	7000
27	DRAMA					1	2,000	8	8000
28	EDUCATION					1	3,000		
29	ENGINEERING					5	4,000		
30	LAW					1	8,000		
31	LIBRARY SCIENCE					1	1,000		
32	MEDICINE					1	8,000		
33	MEDICINE-RELATED PROFESSIONS					6	4,000		
34	MUSIC						0		
35	OCEANOGRAPHY						0		
36	RELIGIOUS STUDIES					1	2,000		
37	SOCIAL WELFARE					1	1,000		
38	VETERINARY SCIENCE						0		
39									
40	M.5: ADDITION FOR UNDERGRADUATE STUDENTS								
41	NUMBER OF UNDERGRADUATE STUDENTS					20,000			
42	RATIO TO 2,000 STUDENTS					7.50			
43	NUMBER OF ADDITIONS						8,000		
44									
45	M.6: ADDITION FOR SPONSORED RESEARCH								
46	TOTAL $ OF GRANTS AND CONTRACTS					30,000,000			
47	RATIO TO $15,000,000					2.00			
48	NUMBER OF ADDITIONS						2,000		
49									
50	M.7: ADDITION FOR LACK OF ACCESS								
51	TRAVEL TIME TO A MAJOR RESEARCH LIBRARY								
52	LESS THAN ONE HOUR (1=YES)								
53	1 TO 2 HOURS (1=YES)					1	10,000		
54	2 OR MORE HOURS (1=YES)					0	0		
55									
56	TOTAL ACQUISITIONS						119,000		

Figure 22. VOIGT: Model to Calculate Acquisition Rates, Example Spreadsheet

In the formula, we first say that IF the value in F29 (the number of engineering programs) is "greater than" three, place the number 4000 in cell G29. But IF cell F29 is equal to zero, place a zero in G29. Finally, IF neither of these conditions is satisfied, multiply the number of programs by 1000. This means that if the number of programs is one, two, or three, they will be multiplied by 1000.

The last formula to be discussed here is the combination of an IF statement and a reference to a LOOKUP table. The operations that take place are even more difficult than the formula would indicate.

Here's what Voigt tells us to do: "For each 2,000 undergraduate students or fraction thereof over 5,000 undergraduate students . . . [add] . . . 1,000" (p. 269). First, we must find out whether or not there are more than 5000 students. If there are, we must calculate how many units of 2000 students there are so that we can multiply this number of units by 1000. (Got that? It's complicated.)

The formula in cell F42 makes this computation: (F41 − 5000)/2000. The formula subtracts 5000 from the total number of students and then divides by 2000. Thus if there are fewer than 5000 students, the resulting number will be a negative number (or less than zero) and no additional acquisitions are necessary. If there are 5000 or more students, the computed number can range from zero (5000 − 5000 divided by 2000 = 0) to any number, depending on the size of the undergraduate student body. The number will be less than 7.5 if you follow my formula, in that I have not extended the computation for schools beyond 20,000 students. (The model must be modified if you have more than 20,000 students. Extend the LOOKUP table in H38 through J45 by incrementing one unit in column H and 1000 units in column J.)

Once we have computed this "ratio" number, we can look it up on a LOOKUP table to see how many additional items should be acquired. Thus the formula in cell G43 reads:

$$IF(F42> =0,LOOKUP(F42,H38:H45),0)$$

We are saying that IF the ratio in cell F42 is greater than or equal to zero, LOOKUP that value in the LOOKUP table that is in H38 through H45 and give the associated value that is in column I. Note that if a value ranges from 2.0 through 2.999, the number 3000 will be transferred. Also, saying that the ratio must be greater than or equal to zero eliminates any negative numbers, and thus schools with fewer than 5000 students will not have any addition. (In fact, that is the purpose of the last 0 in the formula.) This procedure will come in handy whenever you need to increment fractional amounts by some set figure.

Text and Formula Entry (See figure 23, Formula Worksheet)

Columns A through E; Width = 12, Text Left
  Enter the text in columns A and B, with columns C through E as space for spillover.
Column F; Width = 12, Text Right
  Most of the column is used for data entry. However, enter the two formulas in cells F42 and F47.
Column G; Width = 12, Text Right
  Enter the formulas exactly as illustrated. If you need confirmation of the recommended amounts, consult Voigt's article. If you wish to change Voigt's recommendations, you may do so.
Columns H and I: Width = 12, Text Right
  Enter the LOOKUP table values as given. If you need to extend the LOOKUP tables, you will have to insert additional rows on your spreadsheet, beginning at row 45 and at row 56.

Row	Label	F	G	H	I
1	Filename: VOIGT				
2	Date Created:				
3	Date Last Changed:				
4	================				
5	VOIGT ACQUISITIONS MODEL FOR GENERAL UNIVERSITY LIBRARIES				
6	Melvin J. Voigt, "Acquisition Rates in University Libraries", C&RL, 36(4), 1975, pp. 263-271				
7	----				
8	M.1: BASE		40000		
9	M.2: SUBTRACTION				
10	NUMBER OF EUROPEAN LANGUAGE PH.D. PROGRAMS	1	IF(F10=1,1000,(IF(F10=0,2000,0)))		
11	NUMBER OF SOCIAL SCIENCE PH.D. PROGRAMS	5	IF(F11=2,1000,IF(F11=1,2000,IF(F11=0,3000,0)))		
12	PSYCHOLOGY PH.D. (1=YES, 0=NO)	1			
13	PHILOSOPHY PH.D. (1=YES, 0=NO)	0	IF(AND(F12=0,F13=0),1000,0)		
14			SUM(G10:G13)		
15	M.3: ADDITION FOR ADVANCED GRADUATE PROGRAMS				
16	NUMBER OF ADDITIONAL FOREIGN LITERATURE PH.D.'S	2	IF(F16>0,F16 * 2000,0)		
17	SOCIAL SCIENCE PH.D.'S (SEE ABOVE)	5	IF(F17>0,F17 * 2000,0)		
18	EARTH SCIENCE PH.D. PROGRAMS	1	IF(F18>0,F18 * 2000,0)		
19	ASTRONOMY PH.D. PROGRAM	0	IF(F19=1,2000,0)		
20					
21	M.4 ADVANCED GRADUATE AND PROFESSIONAL PROGRAMS				
22	AGRICULTURE	1	IF(F22=1,5000,0)		
23	ARCHITECTURE	1	IF(F23=1,1000,0)		
24	ART	1	IF(F24=1,3000,0)		
25	BUSINESS ADMINISTRATION	1	IF(F25=1,2000,0)		
26	CITY AND REGIONAL PLANNING		IF(F26=1,2000,0)		
27	DRAMA	1	IF(F27=1,2000,0)		
28	EDUCATION	1	IF(F28=1,3000,0)		
29	ENGINEERING	5	IF(F29>3,4000,IF(F29=0,0,F29 * 1000))		
30	LAW	1	IF(F30=1,8000,0)		
31	LIBRARY SCIENCE	1	IF(F31=1,1000,0)		
32	MEDICINE	1	IF(F32=1,8000,0)		
33	MEDICINE-RELATED PROFESSIONS	6	IF(F33>3,4000,IF(F33=0,0,F33 * 1000))		
34	MUSIC		IF(F34=1,3000,0)		
35	OCEANOGRAPHY		IF(F35=1,3000,0)		
36	RELIGIOUS STUDIES	1	IF(F36=1,2000,0)		
37	SOCIAL WELFARE	1	IF(F37=1,1000,0)		
38	VETERINARY SCIENCE		IF(F38=1,2000,0)	0	1000
39				1	2000
40	M.5: ADDITION FOR UNDERGRADUATE STUDENTS			2	3000
41	NUMBER OF UNDERGRADUATE STUDENTS	20000		3	4000
42	RATIO TO 2,000 STUDENTS	(F41-5000)/2000		4	5000
43	NUMBER OF ADDITIONS		IF(F42>=0,LOOKUP(F42,H38:H45),0)	5	6000
44				6	7000
45	M.6: ADDITION FOR SPONSORED RESEARCH			7	8000
46	TOTAL $ OF GRANTS AND CONTRACTS	30000000			
47	RATIO TO $15,000,000	F46/15000000		0	0
48	NUMBER OF ADDITIONS		LOOKUP(F47,H47:H55)	1	1000
49				2	2000
50	M.7: ADDITION FOR LACK OF ACCESS			3	3000
51	TRAVEL TIME TO A MAJOR RESEARCH LIBRARY			4	4000
52	LESS THAN ONE HOUR (1=YES)	1	IF(F52=1,0,0)	5	5000
53	1 TO 2 HOURS (1=YES)		IF(F53=1,10000,0)	6	6000
54	2 OR MORE HOURS (1=YES)	0	IF(F54=1,20000,0)	7	7000
55				8	8000
56	TOTAL ACQUISITIONS		SUM(G8,G15:G54)-G14		

Figure 23.   VOIGT: Model to Calculate Acquisition Rates, Formula Worksheet

Tools for Conducting Special
Output Measures Studies

A great deal of effort has been expended within the American Library Association's Public Library Association to develop measures of library output. The attempt has been to measure the performance of libraries as well as record the existence of resources that could be used by library patrons. The most recent example of this effort is *Output Measures for Public Libraries: A Manual of Standardized Procedures* by Zweizig and Rodger, published by ALA in 1982.[1] *Output Measures* contains twelve summary measures of library performance, as well as the procedures for collecting data for these summary statistics.

In many respects, the concepts embodied in *Output Measures* originated in another ALA publication, *Performance Measures for Public Libraries*.[2] A companion to that volume is *A Data Gathering and Instructional Manual for Performance Measures in Public Libraries*.[3] These early studies led to *A Planning Process for Public Libraries*[4] and *Output Measures for Public Libraries*.

This body of research and investigation has not been implemented very broadly for a number of reasons. In my mind, one major reason is that all these measurement techniques require the processing of extensive amounts of data. The following six spreadsheets are presented as an attempt to lessen this problem by providing a means to help you assemble and calculate the primary data that make up the latest output measures as contained in *Output Measures for Public Libraries*.

You should use the spreadsheets in this section only in conjunction with the detailed explanations in *Output Measures for Public Libraries*. While I will refer to specific sections of that book that deal with individual spreadsheets, I cannot duplicate the explanations of rationale and procedure that the authors have provided. Nevertheless, the six spreadsheets contained here, as well as other spreadsheets in this book, will allow you to calculate most of the summary statistics recommended in *Output Measures*.

INLIB: A Model for Calculating In-Library Materials Use per Capita

The rationale and procedures for studying the use of materials within a library (i.e., materials that are not borrowed for use outside the library) are contained in chapter 2 of *Output Measures for Public Libraries*. Essentially, materials left lying around the

1. Douglas Zweizig and Eleanor Jo Rodger, *Output Measures for Public Libraries: A Manual of Standardized Procedures* (Chicago: ALA, 1982).
2. Ernest DeProspo, Ellen Altman, and Kenneth Beasley with Ellen Connor Clark, *Performance Measures for Public Libraries* (Chicago: ALA, 1973).
3. Ellen Altman, Ernest DeProspo, Ellen Clark, and Philip Clark, *A Data Gathering and Instructional Manual for Performance Measures in Public Libraries* (Chicago: Celadon Press, 1976).
4. Vernon Palmour, Nancy DeWath, and Marcia Bellassi, *A Planning Process for Public Libraries* (Chicago: ALA, 1980).

INLIB

1: Filename:
2: Date Created:
3: Date Last Changed:
4: ================================
5: IN-LIBRARY MATERIALS USE PER CAPITA
6: PLACE SURVEY DAY IN C6   4
7: ------------------------------------

TIME	BOOKS	MAGAZINES	PAMPHLETS	RECORDS	NEWSPAPERS	CONTROLLED MATERIAL	OTHER	TOTAL
10 AM	100	100	30	15	20	10	16	291
11 AM	100	100	30	31	32	15	16	324
12 AM	100	100	31	32	33	18	19	333
1 PM	100	100	32	33	34	19	20	338
2 PM	100	100	33	34	35	14	15	331
3 PM	15	16	34	35	36	16	17	169
4 PM	14	15	10	11	12	12	13	87
5 PM	13	14	10	11	12	14	15	89
6 PM	12	13	10	11	12	17	18	93
7 PM	11	12	10	11	12	19	20	95
8 PM	11	11	10	11	12	20	21	95
9 PM	9	10	10	11	12	21	22	95
TOTAL	584	591	250	246	262	195	212	2340

POP = 34,444

SUMMARY TABLE

TIME	SURVEY DAY 1	SURVEY DAY 2	SURVEY DAY 3	SURVEY DAY 4	SURVEY DAY 5	SURVEY DAY 6	TOTAL	AVERAGE PER DAY	PROJECTED TOTAL/YR	PROJECTED PER CAPITA
10 AM	191	291	291	291	291	191	1,546	258	77,300	2.24
11 AM	189	264	304	324	224	189	1,494	249	74,700	2.17
12 AM	213	263	293	333	233	213	1,548	258	77,400	2.25
1 PM	238	283	278	338	238	238	1,613	269	80,650	2.34
2 PM	306	331	331	331	331	306	1,936	323	96,800	2.81
3 PM	169	169	169	169	169	169	1,014	169	50,700	1.47
4 PM	87	87	87	87	87	87	522	87	26,100	.76
5 PM	89	89	89	89	89	89	534	89	26,700	.78
6 PM	93	93	93	93	93	93	558	93	27,900	.81
7 PM	95	95	95	95	95	95	570	95	28,500	.83
8 PM	95	95	95	95	95	95	570	95	28,500	.83
9 PM	95	95	95	95	95	95	570	95	28,500	.83
TOTAL	1,860	2,155	2,220	2,340	2,040	1,860	12,475	2079	623,750	18.11
AVERAGE/HR	155	180	185	195	170	155	1040	173		
BOOKS	364	459	524	584	459	364	2,754	459	137,700	4.00
MAGAZINES	331	531	531	591	416	331	2,731	455	136,550	3.96
PAMPHLETS	250	250	250	250	250	250	1,500	250	75,000	2.18
RECORDS	246	246	246	246	246	246	1,476	246	73,800	2.14
NEWSPAPERS	262	262	262	262	262	262	1,572	262	78,600	2.28
CONT. MAT.	195	195	195	195	195	195	1,170	195	58,500	1.70
OTHER	212	212	212	212	212	212	1,272	212	63,600	1.85
TOTAL	1,860	2,155	2,220	2,340	2,040	1,860	12,475	2079	623,750	18.11

Figure 24.   INLIB: In-Library Materials Use per Capita, Example Spreadsheet

library are collected, categorized, and tallied once an hour for six days during a recommended sample period. The data collection form is simple in appearance but the computation of the data for all six days may be burdensome if detailed analysis of the results is desired.

Academic libraries can also use this approach for measurement of in-library material use. The headings will have to be changed to reflect the academic library environment. Also, it may be necessary to expand the number of categories to reflect academic use patterns.

General Design Features

The INLIB spreadsheet has two sections (figure 24). The top of the spreadsheet (through row 24) is the daily data collection form. The bottom half of the spreadsheet summarizes the data that are collected each day of the sample time period and calculates the required statistics.

Looking at the formula worksheet (figure 25), you can see that this spreadsheet makes use of what has been termed a *trigger*. The trigger is found in cell C6 and works as follows. When you are working on Survey Day 1, place a 1 in cell C6. When you have completed the daily data entry, the totals are automatically transferred to column B, rows 32 through 56. Before you start to enter the data for Survey Day 2, change the trigger in cell C6 to 2. This will move the totals for that day to column C, rows 32 through 56.

The use of a trigger is very effective in spreadsheets when you wish to have one standard place for data entry but wish to accumulate the totals. It is used in conjunction with an IF statement.

For example, in cell B32 the IF statement reads:

$$IF(C6=1,I11,B32)$$

This formula means that if the trigger in C6 is 1, move the value in I11 (i.e., the total of all material used before 10 a.m.) to this location. But if the trigger is not 1, leave the value in B32 unchanged. This instruction (to leave B32 unchanged) is important because it permits you to transfer the next day's totals to their appropriate positions without changing what you entered for the previous day.

A warning is in order. With this method of using a trigger to accumulate data you also lose the detailed data for each day, unless you SAVE each day's data onto another spreadsheet. If you feel there is a potential need to retrieve (for example) the number of newspapers that were used at 2 p.m. on the fourth survey day, be sure to SAVE each day's data entry portion of INLIB.

Text and Formula Entry (See figure 25, Formula Worksheet)

Column A; Width = 12, Text Left

Enter the text as illustrated.

Enter the long lines in rows 4, 7, 10, 25, 27, and 28, using the REPEAT ENTRY function of your spreadsheet.

Columns B through K; Width = 12, Text Right

Enter the column headings in rows 8 and 9, 26, 29, and 30. Notice that cell G26 is a number, and should be the population of your library's community.

Column B

Enter the SUM formula in cell B24 and REPLICATE it to cells C24 through H24.

Spreadsheet columns: A, B, C, D, E, F, G, H, I, J, K

Row	A	B	C	D	E	F	G	H	I	J	K
1	Filename:		INLIB								
2	Date Created:										
3	Date Last Changed:										
4	============										
5	IN-LIBRARY MATERIALS USE PER CAPITA										
6	PLACE SURVEY DAY IN C6		0								
7	----------										

Table 1

Row	A (TIME)	B (BOOKS)	C (MAGAZINES)	D (PAMPHLETS)	E (RECORDS)	F (NEWSPAPERS)	G (CONTROLLED MATERIAL)	H (OTHER)	I (TOTAL)	J
11	10 AM								SUM(B11:H11)	B24
12	11 AM								SUM(B12:H12)	C24
13	12 AM								SUM(B13:H13)	D24
14	1 PM								SUM(B14:H14)	E24
15	2 PM								SUM(B15:H15)	F24
16	3 PM								SUM(B16:H16)	G24
17	4 PM								SUM(B17:H17)	H24
18	5 PM								SUM(B18:H18)	
19	6 PM								SUM(B19:H19)	
20	7 PM								SUM(B20:H20)	
21	8 PM								SUM(B21:H21)	
22	9 PM								SUM(B22:H22)	
24	TOTAL	SUM(B11:B22)	SUM(C11:C22)	SUM(D11:D22)	SUM(E11:E22)	SUM(F11:F22)	SUM(G11:G22)	SUM(H11:H22)		
25	######	######	######	SUMMARY TABLE ######	######	######	######	######	######	######
26						POP =	34,444			

Table 2

Row	A (TIME)	B (SURVEY DAY 1)	C (SURVEY DAY 2)	D (SURVEY DAY 3)	E (SURVEY DAY 4)	F (SURVEY DAY 5)	G (SURVEY DAY 6)	H (TOTAL)	I (AVERAGE PER DAY)	J (PROJECTED TOTAL/YR)	K (PROJECTED PER CAPITA)
32		IF(C6=1,I11,B32)	IF(C6=2,I11,C32)	IF(C6=3,I11,D32)	IF(C6=4,I11,E32)	IF(C6=5,I11,F32)	IF(C6=6,I11,G32)	SUM(B32:G32)	AVERAGE(B32:G32)	H32*50	J32/G26
33		IF(C6=1,I12,B33)	IF(C6=2,I12,C33)	IF(C6=3,I12,D33)	IF(C6=4,I12,E33)	IF(C6=5,I12,F33)	IF(C6=6,I12,G33)	SUM(B33:G33)	AVERAGE(B33:G33)	H33*50	J33/G26
34		IF(C6=1,I13,B34)	IF(C6=2,I13,C34)	IF(C6=3,I13,D34)	IF(C6=4,I13,E34)	IF(C6=5,I13,F34)	IF(C6=6,I13,G34)	SUM(B34:G34)	AVERAGE(B34:G34)	H34*50	J34/G26
35		IF(C6=1,I14,B35)	IF(C6=2,I14,C35)	IF(C6=3,I14,D35)	IF(C6=4,I14,E35)	IF(C6=5,I14,F35)	IF(C6=6,I14,G35)	SUM(B35:G35)	AVERAGE(B35:G35)	H35*50	J35/G26
36		IF(C6=1,I15,B36)	IF(C6=2,I15,C36)	IF(C6=3,I15,D36)	IF(C6=4,I15,E36)	IF(C6=5,I15,F36)	IF(C6=6,I15,G36)	SUM(B36:G36)	AVERAGE(B36:G36)	H36*50	J36/G26
37		IF(C6=1,I16,B37)	IF(C6=2,I16,C37)	IF(C6=3,I16,D37)	IF(C6=4,I16,E37)	IF(C6=5,I16,F37)	IF(C6=6,I16,G37)	SUM(B37:G37)	AVERAGE(B37:G37)	H37*50	J37/G26
38		IF(C6=1,I17,B38)	IF(C6=2,I17,C38)	IF(C6=3,I17,D38)	IF(C6=4,I17,E38)	IF(C6=5,I17,F38)	IF(C6=6,I17,G38)	SUM(B38:G38)	AVERAGE(B38:G38)	H38*50	J38/G26
39		IF(C6=1,I18,B39)	IF(C6=2,I18,C39)	IF(C6=3,I18,D39)	IF(C6=4,I18,E39)	IF(C6=5,I18,F39)	IF(C6=6,I18,G39)	SUM(B39:G39)	AVERAGE(B39:G39)	H39*50	J39/G26
40		IF(C6=1,I19,B40)	IF(C6=2,I19,C40)	IF(C6=3,I19,D40)	IF(C6=4,I19,E40)	IF(C6=5,I19,F40)	IF(C6=6,I19,G40)	SUM(B40:G40)	AVERAGE(B40:G40)	H40*50	J40/G26
41		IF(C6=1,I20,B41)	IF(C6=2,I20,C41)	IF(C6=3,I20,D41)	IF(C6=4,I20,E41)	IF(C6=5,I20,F41)	IF(C6=6,I20,G41)	SUM(B41:G41)	AVERAGE(B41:G41)	H41*50	J41/G26
42		IF(C6=1,I21,B42)	IF(C6=2,I21,C42)	IF(C6=3,I21,D42)	IF(C6=4,I21,E42)	IF(C6=5,I21,F42)	IF(C6=6,I21,G42)	SUM(B42:G42)	AVERAGE(B42:G42)	H42*50	J42/G26
43		IF(C6=1,I22,B43)	IF(C6=2,I22,C43)	IF(C6=3,I22,D43)	IF(C6=4,I22,E43)	IF(C6=5,I22,F43)	IF(C6=6,I22,G43)	SUM(B43:G43)	AVERAGE(B43:G43)	H43*50	J43/G26
45	TOTAL	SUM(B32:B43)	SUM(C32:C43)	SUM(D32:D43)	SUM(E32:E43)	SUM(F32:F43)	SUM(G32:G43)	SUM(B45:G45)	AVERAGE(B45:G45)	H45*50	J45/G26
46	AVERAGE/HR	AVERAGE(B32:B43)	AVERAGE(C32:C43)	AVERAGE(D32:D43)	AVERAGE(E32:E43)	AVERAGE(F32:F43)	AVERAGE(G32:G43)	SUM(B46:G46)			
48	BOOKS	IF(C6=1,J11,B48)	IF(C6=2,J11,C48)	IF(C6=3,J11,D48)	IF(C6=4,J11,E48)	IF(C6=5,J11,F48)	IF(C6=6,J11,G48)	SUM(B48:G48)	AVERAGE(B48:G48)	H48*50	J48/G26
49	MAGAZINES	IF(C6=1,J12,B49)	IF(C6=2,J12,C49)	IF(C6=3,J12,D49)	IF(C6=4,J12,E49)	IF(C6=5,J12,F49)	IF(C6=6,J12,G49)	SUM(B49:G49)	AVERAGE(B49:G49)	H49*50	J49/G26
50	PAMPHLETS	IF(C6=1,J13,B50)	IF(C6=2,J13,C50)	IF(C6=3,J13,D50)	IF(C6=4,J13,E50)	IF(C6=5,J13,F50)	IF(C6=6,J13,G50)	SUM(B50:G50)	AVERAGE(B50:G50)	H50*50	J50/G26
51	RECORDS	IF(C6=1,J14,B51)	IF(C6=2,J14,C51)	IF(C6=3,J14,D51)	IF(C6=4,J14,E51)	IF(C6=5,J14,F51)	IF(C6=6,J14,G51)	SUM(B51:G51)	AVERAGE(B51:G51)	H51*50	J51/G26
52	NEWSPAPERS	IF(C6=1,J15,B52)	IF(C6=2,J15,C52)	IF(C6=3,J15,D52)	IF(C6=4,J15,E52)	IF(C6=5,J15,F52)	IF(C6=6,J15,G52)	SUM(B52:G52)	AVERAGE(B52:G52)	H52*50	J52/G26
53	CONT. MAT.	IF(C6=1,J16,B53)	IF(C6=2,J16,C53)	IF(C6=3,J16,D53)	IF(C6=4,J16,E53)	IF(C6=5,J16,F53)	IF(C6=6,J16,G53)	SUM(B53:G53)	AVERAGE(B53:G53)	H53*50	J53/G26
54	OTHER	IF(C6=1,J17,B54)	IF(C6=2,J17,C54)	IF(C6=3,J17,D54)	IF(C6=4,J17,E54)	IF(C6=5,J17,F54)	IF(C6=6,J17,G54)	SUM(B54:G54)	AVERAGE(B54:G54)	H54*50	J54/G26
56	TOTAL	SUM(B48:B54)	SUM(C48:C54)	SUM(D48:D54)	SUM(E48:E54)	SUM(F48:F54)	SUM(G48:G54)	SUM(B56:G56)	AVERAGE(B56:G56)	H56*50	J56/G26

Figure 25. INLIB: In-Library Materials Use per Capita, Formula Worksheet

Enter the IF statement formula in cell B32 and REPLICATE it to cells B33 through B43. When replicating, make sure that the reference to cell C6 *does not change.*

Columns C through G

Follow the directions for column B by entering the IF statement formula, replicating the entry to row 43, and making sure that the reference to cell C6 *does not change.*

Column B

Come back to column B and enter the SUM and AVERAGE formulas in cells B45 and B46. REPLICATE these formulas to cells C45 through G45 and C46 through G46.

Enter the IF statement formula in cell B48 and REPLICATE it to cells B49 through B54, making sure that the reference to cell C6 *is not changed.* (Please note: This formula looks for the totals in J11 through J17. These are the column sums in row 24. The purpose of transferring row 24 to column J is to aid in this replication process we have just performed.)

Columns C through G

Follow the directions given immediately above for each of these columns. That is, enter the IF statement formula, replicate it to row 54, and make sure that the reference to cell C6 *is not changed.*

Column B

Back at column B, enter the SUM formula in cell B56.
REPLICATE this formula to cells C56 through G56.

Column H

SUM the six days of data entry by entering the formula in cell H32 and REPLICATE it to H33 through H56.

Column I

Go back to the top of your spreadsheet and enter the SUM formula in cell I11. REPLICATE this formula to cells I12 through I24.

Enter the AVERAGE formula in cell I32 and REPLICATE it to cells I33 through I56.

Column J

Copy the totals that are in row 24 to J11 through J17. As was mentioned earlier, doing this aids in replicating the entries in rows 48 through 54.

Beginning with cell J32, use the formula to "project" the one week of sample data to the entire year. (The authors of *Output Measures* have a rationale for using 50 weeks instead of 52, based on holidays and days closed throughout the year.)

Enter the formula in cell J32 and REPLICATE it to J33 through J56.

Column K

To compute the projected per capita activity for the year, divide the total for the year by the population. Here is where the reference to the population given in G26 is used.

Enter the formula in cell K32 and REPLICATE it to K33 through K56, making sure that the reference to G26 *does not change.*

Clean up the spreadsheet by erasing any formulas in rows 23, 44, 47, and 55. In rows 23, 44, and 55, enter several dashes in column B and REPLICATE the entry to columns C through K.

Using the Model

Follow the data gathering procedures recommended in *Output Measures for Public Libraries* (chapter 2). At the conclusion of the first survey day, set the trigger in cell C6 to 1, enter the data in rows 11 through 22, and the rest of the spreadsheet will automatically be calculated. Move to day 2 and reset the trigger, enter the data, and calculate the totals. Continue this procedure for all six days, *making sure to reset the trigger in C6 before data entry.*

While entering data, turn the automatic calculation feature of your spreadsheet to manual. Otherwise, data entry will be slow because the spreadsheet calculates each entry. When you recalculate, after all the data are entered, do the recalculation twice to assure that all the calculations have been made.

VISITS: A Model to Calculate Library Visits per Capita

Output Measures provides a procedure for estimating the number of visits patrons make to a library each year (see chapter 3). The procedure is based on a count of all individuals who enter the library during one morning, one afternoon, one evening, and one weekend within a week. The figures from this sample period are then projected to month and year totals.

Use the spreadsheet to enter the data collected during the sample time period. All the calculations in the lower half of the spreadsheet will be done automatically (figure 26).

General Design Features

VISITS is a straightforward spreadsheet that uses formulas (see figure 27) for projecting from a small sample of a few days to the entire year. If you collect these data for longer lengths of time than is recommended by *Output Measures*, you can still use the VISITS spreadsheet to do your calculations. For example, you might decide to collect data four times during the year. After all your data are collected, add the total visits for all four mornings and insert the total in cell F10. Total the number of morning hours and insert the total in F15. Then do the same for afternoons, evenings, and weekend time periods. The spreadsheet formulas are designed to take into consideration these additional sample periods. This capability should increase the confidence in the results of those who object to a single sample period.

Text and Formula Entry (See figure 27, Formula Worksheet)

Columns A, B, and C; Width = 12, Text Left
> Enter the text as given. Indentation in this case is handled by moving to column B.

Column E
> The series of dots is entered to assist the eye in moving from the text to the numbers. Use the REPEAT ENTRY function to enter the dots in cell E10 and REPLICATE it to E11 through E49. Later, you can go back and clean up the spreadsheet by erasing or blanking the lines that you do not need.

Column F
> The data from your survey will be entered in column F, rows 10 through 28.
> Enter the formulas in F32 through F49 as given.

```
  :    A    ::    B    ::    C    ::    D    ::    E    ::    F    :
 1 : Filename:              VISITS
 2 : Date Created:
 3 : Date Last Changed:
 4 : ==================================================================
 5 : Estimate of ANNUAL NUMBER OF LIBRARY VISITS
 6 :                                                        RESPOND
 7 :                                                        IN COL F
 8 : - - - - - - - - - - - - - - - - - - - - - - - - - - - - - - - -
 9 : HOW MANY PEOPLE VISITED:
10 :              A. MORNINGS?                 ...............    125
11 :              B. AFTERNOONS?               ...............    250
12 :              C. EVENINGS?                 ...............    220
13 :              D. WEEKENDS?                 ...............    300
14 : HOW MANY HOURS IN EACH SAMPLE PERIOD?
15 :              A. MORNINGS?                 ...............      3
16 :              B. AFTERNOONS?               ...............      5
17 :              C. EVENINGS?                 ...............      4
18 :              D. WEEKENDS?                 ...............      8
19 : HOW MANY HOURS IN THE NORMAL WEEK?
20 :              A. MORNINGS?                 ...............     15
21 :              B. AFTERNOONS?               ...............     25
22 :              C. EVENINGS?                 ...............     20
23 :              D. WEEKENDS?                 ...............      8
24 : HOW MANY PEOPLE ATTENDED PROGRAMS IN
25 :       THE MONTH OF THE SAMPLE?            ...............    250
26 : HOW MANY PEOPLE USED THE MEETING ROOM IN
27 :       THE MONTH OF THE SAMPLE?            ...............    125
28 : POPULATION FOR THE COMMUNITY IS          ............... 34,444
29 :
30 : # # # # # # # # # # # # # # # # # # # # # # # # # # # # # # # # #
31 :
32 : AVERAGE MORNING VISITS/HOUR              ...............     42
33 : AVERAGE AFTERNOON VISITS/HOUR            ...............     50
34 : AVERAGE EVENING VISITS/HOUR              ...............     55
35 : AVERAGE WEEKEND VISITS/HOUR              ...............     38
36 :
37 : ESTIMATED VISITS PER WEEK
38 :              MORNINGS                     ...............    625
39 :              AFTERNOONS                   ...............  1,250
40 :              EVENINGS                     ...............  1,100
41 :              WEEKENDS                     ...............    300
42 :              TOTAL                        ...............  3,275
43 :
44 : ESTIMATED VISITS PER MONTH               ............... 13,755
45 : PLUS PROGRAM ATTENDANCE AND
46 :       USES OF MEETING ROOM               ...............    375
47 : ESTIMATED TOTAL VISITS PER MONTH         ............... 14,130
48 : ESTIMATED TOTAL VISITS PER YEAR          ...............169,560
49 : ESTIMATED VISITS PER CAPITA              ...............   4.92
```

Figure 26. VISITS:
Library Visits per Capita,
Example Spreadsheet

Output Measures does not recommend a sampling procedure to obtain data on program attendance (see chapter 4). Rather, the recommendation is to maintain a log of all programs and attendance for the entire year. The data from this log can be entered into the ACTIVDAY spreadsheet (discussed earlier) or you may record the specifics on this PROGRAM spreadsheet (figure 28).

Using this spreadsheet, you enter the data and description of each program offered to the public. Record attendance by adults and children in columns I and J. At the end of the month, the report at the bottom of the spreadsheet summarizes your activity.

PROGRAM: A Model to Calculate Program Attendance per Capita

Figure 27. VISITS:
Library Visits per Capita,
Formula Worksheet

```
   |      A      ||      B      ||      C      ||      D      ||      E      ||      F      |
 1 | Filename:                     VISITS
 2 | Date Created:
 3 | Date Last Changed:
 4 | ===========================================================================
 5 | Estimate of ANNUAL NUMBER OF LIBRARY VISITS
 6 |                                                                              RESPOND
 7 |                                                                              IN COL F
 8 | - - - - - - - - - - - - - - - - - - - - - - - - - - - - - - - - - - - - - - - - - -
 9 | HOW MANY PEOPLE VISITED:
10 |               A. MORNINGS?                              .................      125
11 |               B. AFTERNOONS?                            .................      250
12 |               C. EVENINGS?                              .................      220
13 |               D. WEEKENDS?                              .................      300
14 | HOW MANY HOURS IN EACH SAMPLE PERIOD?
15 |               A. MORNINGS?                              .................        3
16 |               B. AFTERNOONS?                            .................        5
17 |               C. EVENINGS?                              .................        4
18 |               D. WEEKENDS?                              .................        8
19 | HOW MANY HOURS IN THE NORMAL WEEK?
20 |               A. MORNINGS?                              .................       15
21 |               B. AFTERNOONS?                            .................       25
22 |               C. EVENINGS?                              .................       20
23 |               D. WEEKENDS?                              .................        8
24 | HOW MANY PEOPLE ATTENDED PROGRAMS IN
25 |         THE MONTH OF THE SAMPLE?                        .................      250
26 | HOW MANY PEOPLE USED THE MEETING ROOM IN
27 |         THE MONTH OF THE SAMPLE?                        .................      125
28 | POPULATION FOR THE COMMUNITY IS                        .................    34444
29 |
30 | # # # # # # # # # # # # # # # # # # # # # # # # # # # # # # # # # # # # # # # #
31 |
32 | AVERAGE MORNING VISITS/HOUR                             .................   F10/F15
33 | AVERAGE AFTERNOON VISITS/HOUR                           .................   F11/F16
34 | AVERAGE EVENING VISITS/HOUR                             .................   F12/F17
35 | AVERAGE WEEKEND VISITS/HOUR                             .................   F13/F18
36 |
37 | ESTIMATED VISITS PER WEEK
38 |               MORNINGS                                  .................   F20 * F32
39 |               AFTERNOONS                                .................   F21 * F33
40 |               EVENINGS                                  .................   F22 * F34
41 |               WEEKENDS                                  .................   F23 * F35
42 |               TOTAL                                     .................   SUM(F38:F41)
43 |
44 | ESTIMATED VISITS PER MONTH                              .................   F42 * 4.2
45 | PLUS PROGRAM ATTENDANCE AND
46 |         USES OF MEETING ROOM                            .................   F25+F27
47 | ESTIMATED TOTAL VISITS PER MONTH                        .................   F44+F46
48 | ESTIMATED TOTAL VISITS PER YEAR                         .................   F47 * 12
49 | ESTIMATED VISITS PER CAPITA                             .................   F48/F28
```

The per capita ratio should only be calculated at the end of the year, and is best accomplished by using the capabilities of the ACTIVYR spreadsheet.

General Design Features

PROGRAM uses the COUNT, SUM, and AVERAGE functions of spreadsheets. These are straightforward and have been discussed earlier (e.g., in ACTIVDAY, figure 9).

Perhaps the most useful aspect of the spreadsheet is the record it keeps of the

```
  !  A  !!  B  !!  C  !!  D  !!     E      !!  F  !!  G  !!  H  !!   I   !!   J   !
 1 ! Filename:        PROGRAM
 2 ! Date Created:
 3 ! Date Last Changed:
 4 ! =================================================================
 5 ! PROGRAM ATTENDANCE LOG
 6 ! MONTH OF:        March 1984
 7 ! - - - - - - - - - - - - - - - - - - - - - - - - - - - - - - - - -
 8 ! DATE    NAME OF PROGRAM                                    ADULTS   CHILDREN
 9 !                                                          ATTENDING ATTENDING
10 ! ...............................................................................
11 ! 3/4/84    Income Tax Seminar                                 35
12 ! 3/4/84    Preschool Storyhour                                            18
13 ! 3/6/84    6th grade class visit                                         15
14 ! 3/8/84    Senior Citizen Lunch                               85
15 ! 3/10/84   Spaceship contest                                             35
16 ! 3/15/84   Movie night at the library                         65
17 ! 3/22/84   Tax preparation workshop                           25
18 !
19 !
20 !
21 ! ...............................................................................
22 ! MONTH SUMMARY
23 !
24 ! NUMBER OF ADULT PROGRAMS       =           4
25 ! ADULT ATTENDANCE               =         210
26 ! AVERAGE ADULTS PER PROGRAM     =       52.50
27 ! NUMBER OF JUVENILE PROGRAMS    =           3
28 ! JUVENILE ATTENDANCE            =          68
29 ! AVERAGE JUVENILES PER PROGRAM  =       22.67
30 ! TOTAL PROGRAMS                 =           7
31 ! TOTAL ATTENDANCE               =         213
32 ! AVERAGE PERSONS PER PROGRAM    =       30.43
```

Figure 28. PROGRAM: Program Attendance per Capita, Example Spreadsheet

programs your library offers. You will want to expand the area for entering programs from the ten lines I have provided. For entry of additional programs, move the monthly summary report section from rows 21 through 32 to a place farther down on the spreadsheet. For example, if you expect to have 40 programs a month, rows 21 through 32 would now be rows 51 through 62. The current formula in cell E24 would contain COUNT(I11:I50) and so forth.

Text and Formula Entry (See figure 29, Formula Worksheet)

Columns A, B, and C; Width = 9, Text Left

Enter the text as given. You can continue the "Name of Program" text through column H, if needed.

Enter the long lines in rows 4, 7, 10, and 21, using the REPEAT ENTRY function.

Columns D through J; Width = 9, Text Right

Column E

Enter the formulas as they appear on the formula worksheet.

Column I

Enter the heading for the column. The remainder of the column is used to enter the number of adults who attended each program.

Column J

Enter the heading for the column. The remainder of the column is used to enter the number of children who attended each program.

Figure 29. PROGRAM: Program Attendance per Capita, Formula Worksheet

```
       !  A  !!  B  !!  C  !!  D  !!     E      !! F !! G !! H !!   I   !!   J   !
 1 ! Filename:          PROGRAM
 2 ! Date Created:
 3 ! Date Last Changed:
 4 ! ================================================================
 5 ! PROGRAM ATTENDANCE LOG
 6 ! MONTH OF:        March 1984
 7 ! - - - - - - - - - - - - - - - - - - - - - - - - - - - - - - - - -
 8 ! DATE    NAME OF PROGRAM                                     ADULTS  CHILDREN
 9 !                                                           ATTENDING ATTENDING
10 ! ..............................................................................
11 ! 3/4/84   Income Tax Seminar                                  35
12 ! 3/4/84   Preschool Storyhour                                          18
13 ! 3/6/84   6th grade class visit                                       15
14 ! 3/8/84   Senior Citizen Lunch                                85
15 ! 3/10/84  Spaceship contest                                           35
16 ! 3/15/84  Movie night at the library                         65
17 ! 3/22/84  Tax preparation workshop                           25
18 !
19 !
20 !
21 ! ..............................................................................
22 ! MONTH SUMMARY
23 !
24 ! NUMBER OF ADULT PROGRAMS      =     COUNT(I11:I20)
25 ! ADULT ATTENDANCE              =       SUM(I11:I20)
26 ! AVERAGE ADULTS PER PROGRAM    =   AVERAGE(I11:I20)
27 ! NUMBER OF JUVENILE PROGRAMS   =     COUNT(J11:J20)
28 ! JUVENILE ATTENDANCE           =       SUM(J11:J20)
29 ! AVERAGE JUVENILES PER PROGRAM =   AVERAGE(J11:J20)
30 ! TOTAL PROGRAMS                =        E24+E27
31 ! TOTAL ATTENDANCE              =        E25+E27
32 ! AVERAGE PERSONS PER PROGRAM   =        E31/E30
```

REFER: A Model to Calculate Reference Transactions per Capita and Reference Fill Rate from Sample Data

The measurement of reference activity has occasioned a great deal of study and debate over the years. *Output Measures* suggests two summary statistics to reflect library reference activity. The first is "Reference Transactions per Capita" (see chapter 5), which calculates the ratio of the number of questions asked to the total population. The second is the "Reference Fill Rate" (see chapter 6), which is the ratio of completed questions asked to total questions asked.

If you maintain a log each day of the number of reference and directional questions that your patrons ask, those data can be entered on the ACTIVDAY spreadsheet and the per capita end-of-year total can be calculated on the ACTIVYR spreadsheet. However, if you do not keep a log of all questions asked, you may follow the directions in *Output Measures* to calculate both Reference Transactions per Capita and the Reference Fill Rate. This spreadsheet, REFER (figure 30), includes both measures.

General Design Features

The general procedures suggested in *Output Measures* call for each staff member to maintain a log of questions asked of him or her for one week. The project coordinator must assemble these individual staff logs into a summary report. REFER is designed to assist in that assembly and summarization process. It is not meant to provide comparative data between individual staff members. To perform such a comparison, a much longer sampling period would be required. In effect, the "total line" (row 28) gives the important information for the study.

The general design includes space to record the question-handling activity of four adult reference staff members, three telephone reference staff members, and general

REFER: Reference Transactions Worksheet

	A	B	C	D	E	F	G	H	I	J	K	L	M
1	Filename:			REFER									
2	Date Created:												
3	Date Last Changed:												
4													
5	REFERENCE TRANSACTIONS WORKSHEET												
6									NOT COMPLETED				
7	DEPARTMENT/DIVISION			COMPLETED	REDIRECTED	MATERIAL N/A	MATERIAL N/O	STAFF N/A	OTHER	TOTAL	DIRECTIONAL QUESTIONS	TOTAL TRANSACTIONS	REFERENCE FILL RATE (%)
8													
9													
10	ADULT REFERENCE												
11	STAFF # 1			20	5	2	0	1	0	3	15	28	71.43
12	STAFF # 2			25	2	0	0	2	0	2	20	29	86.21
13	STAFF # 3			5	15	1	0	0	1	2	15	22	22.73
14	STAFF # 4			50	1	0	0	0	0	0	12	51	98.04
15													
16	SUBTOTAL:			100	23	3	0	3	1	7	62	130	76.92
17													
18	TELEPHONE REFERENCE												
19	STAFF # 1			39	15	10	2	15	0	27	20	81	48.15
20	STAFF # 2			20	15	12	10	2	1	25	12	60	33.33
21	STAFF # 3			5	2	0	0	0	0	0	4	7	71.43
22													
23	SUBTOTAL:			64	32	22	12	17	1	52	36	148	43.24
24													
25	MAIL REFERENCE			10	5	0	0	0	0	77	0	92	10.87
26	CHILDREN'S REFERENCE			35	10	12	4	1	1	129	15	174	20.11
27													
28	TOTAL			209	70	37	16	21	3	265	113	544	38.42
29													
30								Jurisdiction Population =				12000	
31								Projected Transactions/Year =				27200	
32								Reference Transactions Per Capita =				2.27	

Figure 30. REFER: Reference Transactions per Capita, Example Spreadsheet

categories for reference questions received by mail and in the children's department. You may have to increase the space for data entry, depending on how many staff are assigned to question-handling activities.

The number of reference transactions per capita is calculated as recommended in *Output Measures*. That is, the total number of reference transactions (see cell L28) is multiplied by 50 weeks (rather than 52 weeks) to arrive at a projected total volume of transactions for the year. This figure is then divided by the jurisdiction population to arrive at the per capita figure.

Text and Formula Entry (See figure 31, Formula Worksheet)

Columns A, B, and C; Width = 12, Text Left

Enter the text as given. The indentation in column A can be done by entering several spaces before typing the text.

Enter the long lines in rows 4, 6, and 9 by using the REPEAT ENTRY function.

Columns D through M; Width = 15, Text Right

Enter the column headings in rows 7 and 8.

Column D

Enter the two SUM formulas in D16 and D23 and the addition formula in cell D28.

REPLICATE each formula to columns E through M.

Column J

Enter the SUM formula in cell J11 and REPLICATE it to cells J12 through J26.

Column L

Enter the addition formula in cell L11 and REPLICATE it to cells L12 through L26.

Column M

Enter the division formula in M11 and REPLICATE it to cells M12 through M28.

Column I

Return to Column I and place the text in cells I29, I30, and I31.

Column L

Move to cell L30 and enter the population of your jurisdiction.

Move to cell L31 and enter the formula to compute the projected transactions for the year.

Move to cell L32 and enter the formula to compute the reference transactions per capita.

Clean up the spreadsheet by blanking or erasing everything from columns D through M in rows 15, 17, 18, 22, 24, and 27. Enter several dashes in cells D15, D22, and D27. REPLICATE these cells to columns E through M.

Using the Model

You should follow the instructions in *Output Measures* for collecting the data during the sample week. Each staff member should maintain a log of questions that are posed to them. Enter each staff member's data in columns D through I. The spreadsheet will calculate all the remaining summary information.

```
A    B    C    D         E          F            G            H       I       J       K            L            M
1 | Filename:
2 | Date Created:
3 | Date Last Changed:
4 | =========================================================================================================
5 | REFERENCE TRANSACTIONS WORKSHEET
6 | ---------------------------------------------------------------------------------------------------------
```

REFER: Reference Transactions Worksheet

Row	DEPARTMENT/DIVISION	COMPLETED (D)	REDIRECTED (E)	NOT COMPLETED — MATERIAL N/A (F)	MATERIAL N/O (G)	STAFF N/A (H)	OTHER (I)	TOTAL (J)	DIRECTIONAL QUESTIONS (K)	TOTAL TRANSACTIONS (L)	REFERENCE FILL RATE (%) (M)
10	ADULT REFERENCE										
11	STAFF # 1	20	5	2	0	1	0	SUM(F11:I11)	15	D11+E11+J11	D11/L11 * 100
12	STAFF # 2	25	2	0	0	2	0	SUM(F12:I12)	20	D12+E12+J12	D12/L12 * 100
13	STAFF # 3	5	15	1	0	0	1	SUM(F13:I13)	15	D13+E13+J13	D13/L13 * 100
14	STAFF # 4	50	1	0	0	0	0	SUM(F14:I14)	12	D14+E14+J14	D14/L14 * 100
15											
16	SUBTOTAL:	SUM(D11:D14)	SUM(E11:E14)	SUM(F11:F14)	SUM(G11:G14)	SUM(H11:H14)	SUM(I11:I14)	SUM(J11:J14)	SUM(K11:K14)	D16+E16+J16	D16/L16 * 100
17											
18	TELEPHONE REFERENCE										
19	STAFF # 1	30	15	10	2	15	0	SUM(F19:I19)	20	D19+E19+J19	D19/L19 * 100
20	STAFF # 2	20	15	12	10	2	1	SUM(F20:I20)	12	D20+E20+J20	D20/L20 * 100
21	STAFF # 3	5	2	0	0	0	0	SUM(F21:I21)	4	D21+E21+J21	D21/L21 * 100
22											
23	SUBTOTAL:	SUM(D19:D21)	SUM(E19:E21)	SUM(F19:F21)	SUM(G19:G21)	SUM(H19:H21)	SUM(I19:I21)	SUM(J19:J21)	SUM(K19:K21)	D23+E23+J23	D23/L23 * 100
24											
25	MAIL REFERENCE	10	5	0	0	0	0	SUM(J20:J23)	0	D25+E25+J25	D25/L25 * 100
26	CHILDREN'S REFERENCE	35	10	12	4	1	1	SUM(J21:J25)	15	D26+E26+J26	D26/L26 * 100
27											
28	TOTAL	D16+D23+D25+D26	E16+E23+E25+E26	F16+F23+F25+F26	G16+G23+G25+G26	H16+H23+H25+H26	I16+I23+I25+I26	J16+J23+J25+J26	K16+K23+K25+K26	L16+L23+L25+L26	D28/L28 * 100

Row		
29		
30	Jurisdiction Population =	12000
31	Projected Transactions/Year =	L28 * 50
32	Reference Transactions Per Capita =	L31/L30

Figure 31. REFER: Reference Transactions per Capita, Formula Worksheet

MATER: A Model to Calculate Materials Availability

Three of the output measures for public libraries rely on a survey form called the Materials Availability Survey (see pp. 65–74 of *Output Measures*). Using this form, you can calculate "Title Fill Rate," "Subject/Author Fill Rate," and "Browsers' Fill Rate." These "fill rate" measures are the ratio of what a patron wanted to obtain to their actual success in obtaining what they wanted.

The MATER spreadsheet (figure 32) also serves as an example of how to record survey data using a spreadsheet program. A different column is used for each possible response to categorical questions. Categorical questions could be a yes or no response to the question "Did you browse through the collection today?" "Yes" responses are tallied in one column and "No" responses in another column.

General Design Features

Two special features of spreadsheet programs are contained in the MATER spreadsheet. First, in column A is a technique that can be used to number a series of rows consecutively within a column. Here you are merely incrementing the number one by one in each row. On a large spreadsheet, this can be very helpful where you want to number a long list sequentially.

Second, spreadsheet users should understand one of the aspects of the COUNT function. That is, it will count all the cells in the range you specify if there is something in each cell. In our example here, we do not wish to count people who did not respond to particular questions. Therefore, we were forced to enter nothing in those cells where they did not respond.

Figure 32. MATER: Materials Availability, Example Spreadsheet

	A	B	C	D	E	F	G
1	Filename:		MATER				
2	Date Created:						
3	Date Last Changed:						
4	==						
5	MATERIALS AVAILABILITY SURVEY						
6	– –						
7	FORM	TITLES	TITLES	SUB/AUTH	SUB/AUTH	BROWSED	BROWSED
8	NUMBER	SOUGHT	FOUND	SOUGHT	FOUND	FOUND	NOT FOUND
9	....						
10	1	2	1	5	4	1	
11	2	2	0	5	4		1
12	3	1	1	5	4		
13	4	5	3	5	4	1	
14	5			5	4		
15	6	2	1				
16	7	2	0	4	3	1	
17	8	1	1	4	3		
18	9	5	3	4	3		
19	10			3	2	1	
20	11	2	1	3	2		1
21	12	2	0	3	2		
22	13	1	1	2	1	1	
23	14	5	3				
24	15			2	1		
25	16	2	1	1	0	1	
26	17	2	0	1	0		
27	18	1	1	1	0		
28	19	5	3	5	4	1	
29	20			5	4		1
30	– –						
31	SUM	40	20	63	45	7	3
32	COUNT	16	16	18	18	7	3
33	....						
34	TITLE FILL RATE (%) =		50				
35	SUBJ/AUTH FILL RATE (%) =		71				
36	BROWSERS' FILL RATE (%) =		70				

For example, in row 14 the individual did not respond to the question about the number of titles sought and found. Therefore, the cells do not contain anything. If we had entered even a zero, the COUNT function would have included it.

Text and Formula Entry (See figure 33, Formula Worksheet)

Column A; Width = 15, Text Left

Enter the text in rows 1 through 9 and rows 30 through 36.

Enter the number 1 in cell A10. Enter the formula A10+1 in cell A11. REPLICATE cells A11 to A12 through A29.

Enter the long lines in rows 4, 6, 9, 30, and 33, using the REPEAT ENTRY function.

Columns B through G; Width = 15, Text Right

Column B

Enter the SUM and COUNT formulas in cells B31 and B32.

REPLICATE these formulas to columns C through G.

Column C

Enter the formulas in cells C34 through C36. Since these are percentages, you must multiply by 100 unless you have an automatic formating function that permits percentaging without multiplying by 100.

	A	B	C	D	E	F	G
1	Filename:		MATER				
2	Date Created:						
3	Date Last Changed:						
4	==						
5	MATERIALS AVAILABILITY SURVEY						
6	– –						
7	FORM	TITLES	TITLES	SUB/AUTH	SUB/AUTH	BROWSED	BROWSED
8	NUMBER	SOUGHT	FOUND	SOUGHT	FOUND	FOUND	NOT FOUND
9	....						
10	1	2	1	5	4	1	
11	A10+1	2	0	5	4		1
12	A11+1	1	1	5	4		
13	A12+1	5	3	5	4	1	
14	A13+1			5	4		
15	A14+1	2	1				
16	A15+1	2	0	4	3	1	
17	A16+1	1	1	4	3		
18	A17+1	5	3	4	3		
19	A18+1			3	2	1	
20	A19+1	2	1	3	2		1
21	A20+1	2	0	3	2		
22	A21+1	1	1	2	1	1	
23	A22+1	5	3				
24	A23+1			2	1		
25	A24+1	2	1	1	0	1	
26	A25+1	2	0	1	0		
27	A26+1	1	1	1	0		
28	A27+1	5	3	5	4	1	
29	A28+1			5	4		1
30	– –						
31	SUM	SUM(B10:B29)	SUM(C10:C29)	SUM(D10:D29)	SUM(E10:E29)	SUM(F10:F29)	SUM(G10:G29)
32	COUNT	COUNT(B10:B29)	COUNT(C10:C29)	COUNT(D10:D29)	COUNT(E10:E29)	COUNT(F10:F29)	COUNT(G10:G29)
33	....						
34	TITLE FILL RATE (%) =		C31/B31 * 100				
35	SUBJ/AUTH FILL RATE (%) =		E31/D31 * 100				
36	BROWSERS' FILL RATE (%) =	F32/(F32+G32) * 100					

Figure 33. MATER: Materials Availability, Formula Worksheet

**OPMSUM: A
Summary Report
on *Output Measures
for Public Libraries***

After you have collected the data for all the output measures, you will want to prepare a summary report of all your activity. A total of 12 measures is contained in the book, and OPMSUM is a table summarizing your results (figure 34).

In this book, spreadsheets have been designed to provide most of the data for this summary report. However, a few measures have not been included. For the most part, they are not calculation models; they are simple tabulations that you should be able to obtain from other files you maintain.

Registration as a percentage of population must come from inspection of your registration files. Once the proper number of registered borrowers has been determined, divide by the population of your jurisdiction.

Turnover rate can be determined by dividing the total circulation at the end of the year by the total number of volumes in your collection. ACTIVYR contains the circulation figures and COLLECT contains the number of volumes held at the end of the year.

Document delivery can also be counted by maintaining a log of requests for materials and the time it takes to fill those requests. Read the instructions in *Output Measures* to learn how to maintain this log of requests.

If you conduct the *Output Measures* study for a series of years, you will be able to analyze the trends that the data suggest. The section on statistical analysis in this book will assist you in the analysis of those trend-line data.

Figure 34. OPMSUM:
Summary Report on
*Output Measures for
Public Libraries*, Example
Spreadsheet

```
    ¦  A  ¦¦  B  ¦¦  C  ¦¦  D  ¦¦  E  ¦¦  F  ¦¦  G  ¦¦  H  ¦¦  I  ¦¦  J  ¦¦  K  ¦
 1 ¦ Filename:        OPMSUM
 2 ¦ Date Created:
 3 ¦ Date Last Changed:
 4 ¦ ================================================================
 5 ¦ OUTPUT MEASURES SUMMARY SHEET
 6 ¦ See Zweizig and Rodger, Output Measures for Public Libraries, ALA, 1982.
 7 ¦ – – – – – – – – – – – – – – – – – – – – – – – – – – – – – – – – – –
 8 ¦ MEASURES                                        RESULT        FROM
 9 ¦ ................................................................
10 ¦  1. CIRCULATIONS PER CAPITA                                    ACTIVYR
11 ¦  2. IN-LIBRARY MATERIALS USE PER CAPITA                        INLIB
12 ¦  3. LIBRARY VISITS PER CAPITA                                  VISITS
13 ¦  4. PROGRAM ATTENDANCE PER CAPITA                              PROGRAM
14 ¦  5. REFERENCE TRANSACTIONS PER CAPITA                          REFER
15 ¦  6. REFERENCE FILL RATE                                        REFER
16 ¦  7. TITLE FILL RATE                                            MATER
17 ¦  8. SUBJECT AND AUTHOR FILL RATE                               MATER
18 ¦  9. BROWSERS' FILL RATE                                        MATER
19 ¦ 10. REGISTRATION AS A PERCENTAGE OF POPULATION                 SPECIAL FORM
20 ¦ 11. TURNOVER RATE                                              ACTIVYR (circulation) and
21 ¦                                                                COLLECT (collection size)
22 ¦ 12. DOCUMENT DELIVERY                                          SPECIAL FORM
23 ¦      A) WITHIN 7 DAYS
24 ¦      B) WITHIN 30 DAYS
```

An Introduction to Statistical Analysis Tools, Using an Electronic Spreadsheet

This section contains eight models designed to allow you to statistically analyze data on other spreadsheets. The models range from a simple descriptive statistics calculation model to a complex correlation and regression model.

Two of the models require study of a standard statistics text; they are the CORREG and XTAB models. The CORREG model deals with correlation and regression, and you should review the rationale behind the calculation of these statistics. The XTAB model includes the chi square statistic, and knowledge of how to interpret that statistic is necessary for the full use of the model.

The other models deal with simple descriptive statistics (DSTAT and FREQ), data manipulation (GROUP and CONTIN), sample-size calculation (SSIZE), and a method to compare libraries (LQ) that I find a very valuable tool.

Obviously, many more statistical tests could be performed on the data you will accumulate over the years. I urge you to follow the general approach I have taken in developing the CORREG and XTAB models; that is, locate computing formulas in standard statistics texts and set up a model on your spreadsheet program.

The statistics text I refer to in the following spreadsheet models is Hubert M. Blalock, Jr., *Social Statistics* (New York: McGraw-Hill, 1960). This is an old edition, but contains especially understandable computing formulas. Blalock is especially good at giving simple examples and illustrating exactly how the computations take place.

DSTAT: A Simple Descriptive Statistics Calculator

There are a number of occasions on which you might want to calculate simple descriptive statistics. For example, you might want to describe, in general terms, the monthly circulation patterns of your library for the past year. Or you might want to see the variation by month of acquisitions of new materials. Other spreadsheets in this book have used several of the built-in functions that are available in spreadsheet programs. The DSTAT spreadsheet (figure 35) combines the statistical functions most readily available into one model.

The most commonly available statistical functions in spreadsheet programs are:

COUNT, which totals the number of nonblank entries in a range of data
SUM, which totals the values of all nonblank entries in a range of data
AVERAGE, which computes the arithmetic mean of the entries in a range of data
MIN (for minimum), which finds the lowest value in the range of data
MAX (for maximum), which finds the highest value in the range of data

Figure 35. DSTAT:
Simple Descriptive
Statistics Calculator,
Example Spreadsheet

```
    !      A       !!      B       !!      C      !
 1 ! Filename:                                DSTAT
 2 ! Date Created:
 3 ! Date Last Changed:
 4 ! ===================================
 5 ! SIMPLE DESCRIPTIVE STATISTICS CALCULATOR
 6 ! -----------------------------------
 7 ! Define X:        PRINT TITLES CATALOGED
 8 ! Describe or number cases in Column A
 9 ! -----------------------------------
10 ! DESCRIPTION                 X           X^2
11 ! -----                    -----        -----
12 ! Jan                        450        202500
13 ! Feb                        500        250000
14 ! Mar                        600        360000
15 ! Apr                        350        122500
16 ! May                        300         90000
17 ! June                       200         40000
18 ! July                       150         22500
19 ! Aug                        150         22500
20 ! Sept                       350        122500
21 ! Oct                        500        250000
22 ! Nov                        650        422500
23 ! Dec                        300         90000
24 ! ......................................
25 ! N =                         12       1995000
26 ! TOTAL =                   4500
27 ! MEAN =                     375
28 ! MAXIMUM =                  650
29 ! MINIMUM =                  150
30 ! STD DEV =          160.078105936
```

An additional measure that is useful for analyzing data is the *standard deviation*. Some spreadsheet programs have this as a built-in function, but a number of the most popular ones do not. In designing DSTAT, a calculating formula for the standard deviation has been included (I have abbreviated it STD DEV).

In the formula for the standard deviation, cell B30, the arithmetic function SQRT is used. This calculates the square root of the number or value in the referenced cell.

As mentioned in the introduction to this section, I have used several of the computing formulas described by Blalock. In this case, the computing formula for the standard deviation can be found in pages 69–70 of that book.

General Design Features

It is wise to fully document any statistical analysis you perform. In figure 35, cell B7 defines what data elements are being analyzed (i.e., Print Titles Cataloged—1983). Here we are also analyzing the month-by-month pattern of cataloging activity.

The spreadsheet can be extended to handle a larger number of data entries. In the example, only 12 data entries are allowed, but by extending the data entry portion to, let us say row 160, we could enter up to 150 data elements. The formulas will have to be adjusted accordingly.

Text and Formula Entry (See figure 36, Formula Worksheet)

Column A; Width = 15, Text Left

Enter the text as indicated. Enter the long lines by using the REPEAT ENTRY function in rows 4, 6, 9, and 24.

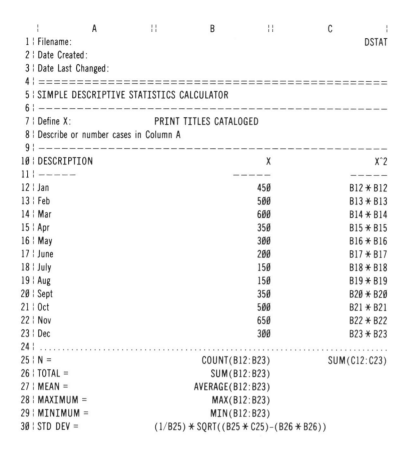

```
   !      A      !!       B      !!       C      !
 1 ! Filename:                                        DSTAT
 2 ! Date Created:
 3 ! Date Last Changed:
 4 ! ================================================
 5 ! SIMPLE DESCRIPTIVE STATISTICS CALCULATOR
 6 ! ------------------------------------------------
 7 ! Define X:              PRINT TITLES CATALOGED
 8 ! Describe or number cases in Column A
 9 ! ------------------------------------------------
10 ! DESCRIPTION                    X              X^2
11 ! -----                        -----          -----
12 ! Jan                           450          B12 * B12
13 ! Feb                           500          B13 * B13
14 ! Mar                           600          B14 * B14
15 ! Apr                           350          B15 * B15
16 ! May                           300          B16 * B16
17 ! June                          200          B17 * B17
18 ! July                          150          B18 * B18
19 ! Aug                           150          B19 * B19
20 ! Sept                          350          B20 * B20
21 ! Oct                           500          B21 * B21
22 ! Nov                           650          B22 * B22
23 ! Dec                           300          B23 * B23
24 ! ...............................................
25 ! N =                    COUNT(B12:B23)    SUM(C12:C23)
26 ! TOTAL =                 SUM(B12:B23)
27 ! MEAN =                AVERAGE(B12:B23)
28 ! MAXIMUM =               MAX(B12:B23)
29 ! MINIMUM =               MIN(B12:B23)
30 ! STD DEV =      (1/B25) * SQRT((B25 * C25)-(B26 * B26))
```

Figure 36. DSTAT: Simple Descriptive Statistics Calculator, Formula Worksheet

Column B; Width = 15, Text Right
Enter the formulas in cells B25 through B30. The left and right parentheses in the standard deviation formula (cell B30) are very important. Make sure there are the same number of left parentheses as right parentheses.
Format row 7 to Text Left.

Column C; Width = 15, Text Right
This column is used to square the value of X, which is calculated by multiplying the value by itself. You may also use the squaring function, such as B12^2, but some spreadsheet programs slow down when this notation is used.
Enter the first formula in cell C12 and REPLICATE that cell to cells C13 through C23.
Enter the SUM formula in cell C25. This is the sum-of-squares formula.

CORREG: A Correlation and Regression Model

A much-used statistical technique for studying time series data (i.e., changes in activities or actions from month to month or year to year) is termed *linear regression* by statisticians. In effect, the analysis attempts to predict the short-term future from events of the past. For example, we might want to predict circulation three years from now, based on the pattern of circulation for the past 8 to 10 years.

Regression analysis can be performed by using a single variable, such as circulation, expenditures for materials, staff hours worked, and the like. In addition, you may wish to study the relationship between two variables, such as (a) circulation and (b) total materials owned. Not only are you interested in what the short-term future might hold

	A	B	C	D	E	F	G	H	I	J	K	L	M	N
1:	Filename:	CORREG												
2:	Date Created:													
3:	Date Last Changed:													
4:	==========													
5:	CORRELATION AND REGRESSION CALCULATOR													
6:	ENTER DATA IN ROWS 12 & 13													
7:														
8:	Define Your Variables													
9:	X is:	Total Library Expenses (000's)												
10:	Y is:	Year Expended												
11:														
12:	X		456	430	440	480	495	500	495	490	505	515		
13:	Y		1975	1976	1977	1978	1979	1980	1981	1982	1983	1984		
14:														
15:	X^2		207936	184900	193600	230400	245025	250000	245025	240100	255025	265225	0	0
16:	Y^2		3900625	3904576	3908529	3912484	3916441	3920400	3924361	3928324	3932289	3936256	0	0
17:	X*Y		900600	849680	869880	949440	979605	990000	980595	971180	1001415	1021760	0	0
18:														
19:	N (X) =	10			AVERAGE X =	480.6								
20:	N (Y) =	10			AVERAGE Y =	1979.5								
21:	SUM X =	4806			MINIMUM X =	430								
22:	SUM Y =	19795			MAXIMUM X =	515								
23:	SUM X^2 =	2317236			MINIMUM Y =	1975								
24:	SUM Y^2 =	39184285			MAXIMUM Y =	1984								
25:	SUM X*Y =	9514155												
26:	SD (X) =	27.33569												
27:	SD (Y) =	2.872281												
28:														
29:	Correlation and Regression													
30:														
31:	Correlation (r)				.8635205									
32:	% Variation Explained (r^2)				74.56677									
33:														
34:	Linear Regression													
35:	For a & b in the formula: Y = a + bX													
36:	b =	.0907339												
37:	a =	1935.893												
38:	To predict Y, place X in E38				650									
39:	Y =				1994.870									
40:	To predict X, place Y in E41				1987									
41:	X =				563.2593									

Figure 37. CORREG: Correlation and Regression Model, Example Spreadsheet

for each of these variables, but you also wish to see the strength of the relationship between them. Thus, does circulation rise as materials owned rise? The statistic that gives us this information is the correlation coefficient (r).

The CORREG spreadsheet (figure 37) is designed to calculate the descriptive statistics contained in DSTAT—as well as a measure of correlation and regression. It can be used with a single variable by blanking all entries in the Y row (row 13) or it can be used to calculate the correlation coefficient (see cell E31), and, if the correlation is sufficiently large, to predict any values of either X given Y or Y given X.

A necessary caution: Use of this powerful tool assumes a knowledge of statistics. I urge you to study a standard statistics book, after you have constructed the spreadsheet, to understand what is really happening in the calculations. With such study and an ability to calculate the statistics easily with this model, you should develop a proper appreciation of the usefulness *and* limitations of this method.

General Design Features

Rows 9 and 10 are used to insert descriptive titles for the variables you will be studying. The entry of the data you wish to analyze is made in rows 12 and 13. All other calculations are done automatically by the model.

Six basic figures are needed for the calculation of the correlation and regression statistics:

1. N: total number of paired entries
2. SUM of X: sum of the X entries
3. SUM of Y: sum of the Y entries
4. SUM of X^2: sum of the squares of the X entries
5. SUM of Y^2: sum of the squares of the Y entries
6. SUM $X*Y$: sum of each X multiplied by its paired Y

The standard deviation for each variable has also been incorporated into the spreadsheet, with the result that you have a fairly complete statistics calculator on one spreadsheet.

The SUMS (2 through 6 above) are accumulated in column A, cells 19 through 25. The formula for calculating the correlation coefficient is extremely lengthy and must be entered exactly as written, including all the parentheses. Here is the computational formula that is entered in cell E31:

(((B19*B25))−(B21*B22))/SQRT(((B19*B23)−(B21*B21))*((B19*B24)−(B22*B22)))

The actual statistical formula is written as follows:

$$\frac{N(\Sigma XY)-(\Sigma X)(\Sigma Y)}{\sqrt{[N(\Sigma X^2)-(\Sigma X)^2][N(\Sigma Y^2)-(\Sigma Y)^2]}}$$

(See Blalock, p. 289.) All that has been done with the computational formula is to substitute the cell references for the statistical labels. Thus B19 is N, B25 is sumX*Y, and so on.

With care and practice, you should be able to take a variety of statistical formulas from standard texts and convert them into spreadsheet references. The key is to assemble all the parts of the formula in one location (here, cells B19 through B25) and then construct the actual computing formula, such as the correlation formula in cell E31 which references those summary cells.

One simple method for interpreting the correlation coefficient is to square it. When squared, it represents "the proportion of the total variation in the one variable explained by the other" (Blalock, p. 298). In our example spreadsheet, the correlation coefficient of .8635205 explains about 75 percent of the variation. Unless the correlation is above .700, less than 50 percent of the variation is explained. Thus r^2, included in E32, is a sensible check on what might be interpreted as significant correlations.

The regression equation is calculated in rows 35 through 41. The linear equation is $Y = a + bX$, using the least-squares method. The statistical formulas for determining a and b (which allows us to compute Y, given a value of X, and X, given a value of Y) are:

$$b = \frac{N(\Sigma XY) - (\Sigma X)(\Sigma Y)}{N(\Sigma X^2) - (\Sigma X)^2}$$

$$a = \frac{(\Sigma Y) - b(\Sigma X)}{N}$$

Substituting our cell references, we have the following computational formulas:

b = ((B19∗B25)−(B21∗B22))/((B19∗B23)−(B21∗B21)) entered in cell B36.

a = (B22−(B36∗B21))/B19 entered in cell B37.

In order to solve for Y in the equation $Y = a + bX$, we enter our spreadsheet formula as: B37+(B36∗E38).

But in order to solve for X in the equation $Y = a + bX$, we convert the formula to read:

$$X = \frac{Y - a}{b}$$

Thus our spreadsheet formula in E41 is (E40−B37)/B36.

The end result of all this effort is that if your correlation coefficient is reasonably high, say over .7, and explains more than 50 percent of the variation, you could enter any value of X in cell E38 and the predicted value of Y would be displayed in cell E39. Similarly, you could compute values of X, given a value of Y.

In figure 38, if we wanted to predict in what year expenses would total $650,000, we would enter 650 (because we are rounding to the nearest thousand) in cell E38, and the prediction would be that it would happen in 1994.870, or about 1994. Similarly, we can insert the year 1985 as the Y value in E40 and it would predict expenses of about $563,259 in that year.

Text and Formula Entry (See figure 38, Formula Worksheet)

Column A; Width = 9, Text Left

Enter the text as shown. You may use columns B through D for much of the text in rows 29 through 41 if your spreadsheet allows spillover titles. If it does not, format columns A through D as Text Left.

Columns B through N; Width = 9, Text Left

Column B

Enter the formula B12∗B12 in cell B15. REPLICATE it to cells C15 through N15.

Do the same for cells B16 and B17.

	A	B	C	D	E	F	G	H	I	J	K	L	M	N
1	Filename:													
2	Date Created:													
3	Date Last Changed:													
4	===		CORREG											
5	CORRELATION AND REGRESSION CALCULATOR													
6	ENTER DATA IN ROWS 12 & 13													
7														
8	Define Your Variables													
9	X is:	Total Library Expenses (000's)												
10	Y is:	Year Expended												
11														
12	X	456	430	440	480	495	500	495	490	505	515			
13	Y	1975	1976	1977	1978	1979	1980	1981	1982	1983	1984			
14														
15	X^2	B12*B12	C12*C12	D12*D12	E12*E12	F12*F12	G12*G12	H12*H12	I12*I12	J12*J12	K12*K12	L12*L12	M12*M12	N12*N12
16	Y^2	B13*B13	C13*C13	D13*D13	E13*E13	F13*F13	G13*G13	H13*H13	I13*I13	J13*J13	K13*K13	L13*L13	M13*M13	N13*N13
17	X*Y	B12*B13	C12*C13	D12*D13	E12*E13	F12*F13	G12*G13	H12*H13	I12*I13	J12*J13	K12*K13	L12*L13	M12*M13	N12*N13
18														
19	N (X) =	COUNT(B12:N12)		AVERAGE X =	AVERAGE(B12:N12)									
20	N (Y) =	COUNT(B13:N13)		AVERAGE Y =	AVERAGE(B13:N13)									
21	SUM X =	SUM(B12:N12)		MINIMUM X =	MIN(B12:N12)									
22	SUM Y =	SUM(B13:N13)		MAXIMUM X =	MAX(B12:N12)									
23	SUM X^2 =	SUM(B15:N15)		MINIMUM Y =	MIN(B13:N13)									
24	SUM Y^2 =	SUM(B16:N16)		MAXIMUM Y =	MAX(B13:N13)									
25	SUM X*Y =	SUM(B17:N17)												
26	SD (X) =	(1/B19)*SQRT((B19*B23)-(B21*B21))												
27	SD (Y) =	(1/B20)*SQRT((B20*B24)-(B22*B22))												
28														
29	Correlation and Regression													
30														
31	Correlation (r)				((B19*B25)-(B21*B22))/SQRT(((B19*B23)-(B21*B21))*((B19*B24)-(B22*B22)))									
32	% Variation Explained (r^2)				(E31*E31)*100									
33														
34	Linear Regression													
35	For a & b in the formula: Y = a + bX													
36	b =	((B19*B25)-(B21*B22))/((B19*B23)-(B21*B21))												
37	a =	(B22-(B36*B21))/B19												
38	To predict Y, place X in E38				650									
39	Y = ...				B37+(B36*E38)									
40	To predict X, place Y in E41				1987									
41	X = ...				(E40-B37)/B36									

Figure 38. CORREG: Correlation and Regression Model, Formula Worksheet

Column C
Enter the formulas as given in cells B19 through B27 and B36 and B37.
Column D
Enter, as text, the descriptions in D19 through D24.
Column E
Take extreme care to enter the correlation formula in cell E31. Then enter the three other formulas in E32, E39, and E41.
Column F
Enter the formulas in cells F19 through F24.

Using the Model

This discussion has detailed the use of the correlation and regression model. If 13 entries are not sufficient (and they often will not be), use this spreadsheet as an example to construct a much larger one. You can continue the data entry another 40 or more columns. All you need do is change the references to column N in cells B19 through B25 to the last column you will be using. You must also REPLICATE the formulas in rows 15 through 17 to that last column. Warm-Up Exercise 8 gives hints on how to modify spreadsheets.

To make an even larger spreadsheet with room for more data, redesign the spreadsheet so that the data entry goes down rather than across. Rows 12 through 17 would become columns. You should be able to enter at least 120 pairs of data observations if you have at least 23K of working space in your spreadsheet program.

Finally, if you run out of space in trying to develop a large spreadsheet, SAVE the values in cells B19 through B25 into another spreadsheet. Then BLANK your data entries and enter the rest of your data entries. Add the results of the second pass to those of the first pass. Then enter the new totals as values, in place of the formulas in B19 through B25. The new statistics for correlation and regression will be calculated.

With this method, you could—potentially—analyze any number of entries (but it will be time consuming).

FREQ: A Model to Generate Frequency Distributions

The vast majority of spreadsheet models in this book are concerned with the analysis of what is termed *continuous* data. The data are in the form of an absolute or ratio score, such as dollars, or materials purchased, or activities undertaken. The range of the data can be from nothing to millions, including anything in between.

Grouped data (such as responses to one of several categories on a questionnaire) or different groupings of patrons (such as children, young adults, adults, and senior adults) have different characteristics and must be handled differently. Grouped data are generally nominal level or interval level, and cannot be described or analyzed using correlation and regression techniques.

The four spreadsheets—FREQ, GROUP, CONTIN, and XTAB—allow you to describe and analyze such data. They are of greatest use in analyzing survey questionnaires, such as short user questionnaires handed out to patrons who enter a building or evaluations of programs by attendees. The survey instruments in *A Planning Process for Public Libraries* could be analyzed by using these models as well.

In terms of spreadsheet programming techniques (model building), the spreadsheets illustrate the use of several different types of formulas. The FREQ spreadsheet (figure 39) is a convenient way to study the use of IF statements. The GROUP spreadsheet makes a novel use of the LOOKUP function. CONTIN uses AND statements (one of the few references to this Boolean operator in the book). Finally, the XTAB spreadsheet draws upon the results of CONTIN to present a detailed cross-tabulation and percentage table, as well as the calculation of the chi-square statistic.

```
     :    A      ::    B     ::    C     ::    D     :
 1 : Filename:                    FREQ
 2 : Date Created:
 3 : Date Last Changed:
 4 : =========================================
 5 : FREQUENCY TABLE GENERATOR
 6 : ------------------------------------------
 7 : RESPONSE          SATISFIED      NEUTRAL    DISSATISFIED
 8 : CODE                  1             2            3
 9 : ------------------------------------------
10 : 1                     1             0            0
11 : 2                     0             1            0
12 : 2                     0             1            0
13 : 1                     1             0            0
14 : 3                     0             0            1
15 : 3                     0             0            1
16 : 2                     0             1            0
17 : 1                     1             0            0
18 : 1                     1             0            0
19 : 1                     1             0            0
20 : 2                     0             1            0
21 : 1                     1             0            0
22 :                 ------------------------------
23 :                       6             4            2
24 :
25 :
26 : SUMMARY              NUMBER       PERCENT
27 :
28 : SATISFIED             6            50.00
29 : NEUTRAL               4            33.33
30 : DISSATISFIED          2            16.67
31 :                      ----         ------
32 : TOTAL                 12          100.00
```

Figure 39. FREQ:
Model to Generate
Frequency Distributions,
Example Spreadsheet

Frequency Distributions

Surprisingly, construction of frequency distributions is not the easiest function of spreadsheet programs. A frequency distribution describes, for example, how many individuals responded yes to a question and how many responded no to that question. Or you might be interested in knowing how many individuals were satisfied with their library visit, how many were dissatisfied, and how many were neutral (i.e., neither satisfied nor dissatisfied). Typically in survey analysis, we code each response with a number. In this case, "satisfied" would be coded 1, "neutral" would be coded 2, and "dissatisfied" would be coded 3. The problem is to count the number of 1s, 2s and 3s.

If you are a somewhat experienced "spreadsheeter," you might solve the problem by merely placing all 1s in (for example) column B, all 2s in column C, and all 3s in column D. Then you would use the COUNT function to see the number of entries in each column.

This is a viable solution. But it is time consuming to move from column to column to enter the data. Use of the IF statement allows you to place all the responses in one column and total them in other columns.

General Design Features

Formulas that use IF statements in FREQ are much like those used in the DISBMO spreadsheet (presented earlier). An IF statement such as IF(A10=B8,1,0) says that if the number in cell A10 is the same as the number in cell B8, place a 1 in this cell; otherwise, place a zero in this cell. This allows all data entry to be in a single column, with the other columns used as accumulation registers.

When all the questionnaire responses have been entered, the SUM functions in row 23 add up the number of 1s in each column. You cannot use the COUNT function because there are formulas in each cell of each column. COUNT sees each cell as occupied and thus "counts" it. However, SUM sees only the numbers that have been entered and because all are 1s, it performs a type of counting function.

At the bottom of the spreadsheet, accumulate the sums into a report table. The percentage for each category can also be calculated here.

Text and Formula Entry (See figure 40, Formula Worksheet)

Column A; Width = 12, Text Left

Enter the text in rows 1 through 9 and rows 26 through 32.

Right justify the text in rows 7 and 8 and 26 through 32.

Note that the numbers in B8, C8 and D8 are values.

Cells A10 through A21 in the example are used to enter the response codes for each question.

Columns B through D; Width = 12, Text Right

Enter the formula in cell B10. REPLICATE B10 to C10 and D10, making sure that the reference to A10 *does not change*.

REPLICATE B10 to B11 through B21, making sure that the reference to B8 *does not change*.

REPLICATE C10 to C11 through C21, making sure that the reference to C8 *does not change*.

Figure 40. FREQ: Model to Generate Frequency Distributions, Formula Worksheet

	A	B	C	D
1	Filename:		FREQ	
2	Date Created:			
3	Date Last Changed:			
4	==			
5	FREQUENCY TABLE GENERATOR			
6	--			
7	RESPONSE	SATISFIED	NEUTRAL	DISSATISFIED
8	CODE	1	2	3
9	--			
10	1	IF(A10=B8,1,0)	IF(A10=C8,1,0)	IF(A10=D8,1,0)
11	2	IF(A11=B8,1,0)	IF(A11=C8,1,0)	IF(A11=D8,1,0)
12	2	IF(A12=B8,1,0)	IF(A12=C8,1,0)	IF(A12=D8,1,0)
13	1	IF(A13=B8,1,0)	IF(A13=C8,1,0)	IF(A13=D8,1,0)
14	3	IF(A14=B8,1,0)	IF(A14=C8,1,0)	IF(A14=D8,1,0)
15	3	IF(A15=B8,1,0)	IF(A15=C8,1,0)	IF(A15=D8,1,0)
16	2	IF(A16=B8,1,0)	IF(A16=C8,1,0)	IF(A16=D8,1,0)
17	1	IF(A17=B8,1,0)	IF(A17=C8,1,0)	IF(A17=D8,1,0)
18	1	IF(A18=B8,1,0)	IF(A18=C8,1,0)	IF(A18=D8,1,0)
19	1	IF(A19=B8,1,0)	IF(A19=C8,1,0)	IF(A19=D8,1,0)
20	2	IF(A20=B8,1,0)	IF(A20=C8,1,0)	IF(A20=D8,1,0)
21	1	IF(A21=B8,1,0)	IF(A21=C8,1,0)	IF(A21=D8,1,0)
22		--		
23		SUM(B10:B21)	SUM(C10:C21)	SUM(D10:D21)
24				
25				
26	SUMMARY	NUMBER	PERCENT	
27				
28	SATISFIED	B23	B28/B32 * 100	
29	NEUTRAL	C23	B29/B32 * 100	
30	DISSATISFIED	D23	B30/B32 * 100	
31		----	------	
32	TOTAL	SUM(B28:B30)	B32/B32 * 100	

REPLICATE D10 to D11 through D21, making sure that the reference to D8 *does not change*.

Enter the SUM formula in cell B23. REPLICATE cell B23 to C23 and D23.

Enter the three cell references in cells B23 through B30 and the SUM formula in cell B32.

Enter the calculating formula for the percent in cell C28 and REPLICATE it to C29 through C32.

Enter the short underscored lines in row 31.

Using the Model

For practical use of the model, FREQ will have to be extended to allow for many more rows of data entry. You should be able to extend the data-entry portion to allow for up to 150 questionnaires. Do it by replicating down each column the desired number of rows. Then, when entering the SUM formulas in row 23, change the reference to the last row of IF statements. Adjust the references in the report portion to reflect the new SUMs.

If you have more than 150 or so rows, you may have to SAVE the results after you completely fill the spreadsheet. Transfer the totals (as numbers) to a new row at the bottom of this spreadsheet. Then BLANK all your data entries for the first group of responses. Now enter the remaining data entries. Transfer those totals to another new row in the spreadsheet. Then add the two new rows together to arrive at a new, combined total. Feed these results into your report and you have a summary of all the cases in your study.

In this way you can handle many more cases than your spreadsheet might permit, due to its memory limitations. This technique can be used with other models in this section, such as CORREG, GROUP, and CONTIN.

GROUP: A Model to Create Grouped Data from Continuous Data

Often, for purposes of clarity of presentation, it is desirable to group continuous data. One example would be to take the total expenditures of all libraries in a state and group them into five categories. Or you may want to group the ages of people who responded to a questionnaire into categories such as young, middle aged, and elderly.

While continuous data can be analyzed using the DSTAT and CORREG spreadsheets, you may want to categorize the data as well. This can be done by using IF statements of the type "IF expenditures are greater than a certain amount but less than another amount, code the library as 1," and so on. But here I have used the LOOKUP function of the spreadsheet to perform the same thing, without the bother of complicated IF statements.

General Design Features

In GROUP (figure 41), five categories of total expenditures are used:

1. $1 through $24,999
2. $25,000 through $49,999
3. $50,000 through $99,999
4. $100,000 through $249,999
5. $250,000 and greater

Figure 41. GROUP:
Model to Create Grouped
Data from Continuous
Data, Example
Spreadsheet

```
     ¦      A      ¦¦      B      ¦¦      C      ¦¦      D      ¦
 1 ¦ Filename:                                GROUP
 2 ¦ Date Created:
 3 ¦ Date Last Changed:
 4 ¦ ================================================
 5 ¦ GROUPED DATA FROM CONTINUOUS DATA TEMPLATE
 6 ¦ ------------------------------------------------
 7 ¦ CONTINUOUS              GROUPED         LOOKUP
 8 ¦ DATA                    DATA            TABLE
 9 ¦ (EXPENDITURES)          (CODE)    (EXPENDITURES)          (CODE)
10 ¦ ...............................................
11 ¦          $65,000           3              $1              1
12 ¦         $175,000           4          $25,000            2
13 ¦          $15,000           1          $50,000            3
14 ¦          $99,999           3         $100,000            4
15 ¦         $750,000           5         $250,000            5
16 ¦          $24,000           1
17 ¦          $32,000           2
18 ¦         $224,000           4
19 ¦         $650,000           5
20 ¦          $43,000           2
```

If a library's expenditures are $65,000, we want to assign it to category 3, or if the expenditures are $175,000 it should be assigned to category 4. The LOOKUP function of spreadsheet programs provides this capability.

In column C we have placed the beginning points for each category. If the expenditures are equal to this amount or less than the amount in the next category, it will enter the number that is in column D.

The first LOOKUP formula in cell B11 is

$$LOOKUP(A11,C11:C15)$$

Translated, it says to look at the number in cell A11 and compare it to the numbers in cells C11 through C15. Normally, it would be looking for an exact match between the two numbers. But the LOOKUP function operates in such a way that, if an exact match is not found, it assumes that all values from the one listed to the next listed value fall in that category. This allows you to categorize raw numbers.

Once the continuous data have been coded using GROUP, you can transfer the coded data to the FREQ spreadsheet to analyze it. Or you could combine GROUP with FREQ in order to group the data, then prepare a frequency distribution.

Text and Formula Entry (See figure 42, Formula Worksheet)

Column A; Width = 15, Text Left (If possible, format the data entry portion to Text Right)

Enter the text and headings in rows 1 through 10. Use the REPEAT ENTRY function to insert the long lines.

Column B

Enter the LOOKUP formula in cell B11. REPLICATE B11 to B12 through B20, making sure that you *do not change* the references to C11 and C15.

Column C

Enter the categories that will be looked up. Each number entered will be the beginning point in the category.

Column D

Enter the codes that you are assigning to each category.

```
    !   A   !!       B        !!    C    !!    D    !
 1 ! Filename:                            GROUP
 2 ! Date Created:
 3 ! Date Last Changed:
 4 ! ===============================================
 5 ! GROUPED DATA FROM CONTINUOUS DATA TEMPLATE
 6 ! -----------------------------------------------
 7 ! CONTINUOUS              GROUPED        LOOKUP
 8 ! DATA                    DATA           TABLE
 9 ! (EXPENDITURES)          (CODE)    (EXPENDITURES)     (CODE)
10 ! .........................................................
11 !         65000    LOOKUP(A11,C11:C15)          1         1
12 !        175000    LOOKUP(A12,C11:C15)      25000         2
13 !         15000    LOOKUP(A13,C11:C15)      50000         3
14 !         99999    LOOKUP(A14,C11:C15)     100000         4
15 !        750000    LOOKUP(A15,C11:C15)     250000         5
16 !         24000    LOOKUP(A16,C11:C15)
17 !         32000    LOOKUP(A17,C11:C15)
18 !        224000    LOOKUP(A18,C11:C15)
19 !        650000    LOOKUP(A19,C11:C15)
20 !         43000    LOOKUP(A20,C11:C15)
```

Figure 42. GROUP: Model to Create Grouped Data from Continuous Data, Formula Worksheet

Using the Model

You can extend this spreadsheet to as many rows as your spreadsheet program can handle. Just continue the replication to as many rows as you need. (See Warm-Up Exercise 8 for hints on this procedure.)

CONTIN: A Model for Constructing Contingency Tables

In most social science research, we wish to study the relationship between two or more variables. If our data are continuous, we can use the correlation and regression techniques illustrated in the spreadsheet CORREG. However, if the data are grouped, you must analyze the data using different techniques.

The development of contingency tables or cross-tabulations is common in survey research. Perhaps you wish to see how persons of different gender respond to a question on their use of a library. Or you may wish to study the differences between the five categories of libraries (established in the GROUP spreadsheet) on the types of benefit programs they provide their employees.

The contingency table you must construct is illustrated at the bottom of the example spreadsheet, where the responses of men and women are compared to their reported use of a library. First, you must code each response to the gender and use questions. For example, women would be coded number 1 and men number 2. Reported heavy use is coded 1, medium use is coded 2, and light use is coded 3. Now you must draw these responses together so that you can say a certain number of women said they were heavy users or a certain number of men said they were light users, and so forth.

Every possible combination of gender and use must be included. To find the number of possible combinations, multiply the number of categories of the first variable (gender) by the number of categories of the second variable (use). In this example, there are six possible combinations of response. The total combinations are the number of cells in our contingency table.

Here are the possible combinations of the codes that are assigned to gender and use:

Figure 43. CONTIN:
Model for Constructing
Contingency Tables,
Example Spreadsheet

	A	B	C	D	E	F	G	H
1	Filename:		CONTIN					
2	Date Created:							
3	Date Last Changed:							
4	==							
5	CONTINGENCY TABLE CONSTRUCTION TEMPLATE							
6	Matches two sets of coded values for a two by three table							
7	- -							
8	Gender	Use	Cell A	Cell B	Cell C	Cell D	Cell E	Cell F
9	- -							
10	2	2	0	0	0	1	0	0
11	1	3	0	0	0	0	1	0
12	1	1	1	0	0	0	0	0
13	2	1	0	1	0	0	0	0
14	1	2	0	0	1	0	0	0
15	1	1	1	0	0	0	0	0
16	2	3	0	0	0	0	0	1
17	1	1	1	0	0	0	0	0
18	1	1	1	0	0	0	0	0
19	2	3	0	0	0	0	0	1
20	2	1	0	1	0	0	0	0
21	1	3	0	0	0	0	1	0
22			===					
23			4	2	1	1	2	2
24			....					
25			WOMEN	MEN				
26								
27		HEAVY USE	4	2				
28		MEDIUM USE	1	1				
29		LIGHT USE	2	2				

	Women (1)	Men (2)
(1) Heavy use	1,1	2,1
(2) Medium use	1,2	2,2
(3) Light use	1,3	2,3

General Design Features

If there are six possible combinations in your contingency table, you must allow six columns for the accumulation of the data. In the example, a combination of 1,1 (women who are heavy users) goes into column C; a combination of 1,2 (men who are heavy users) goes into column D; and so on.

If you wish to analyze contingency tables which are larger or smaller than the example, you must calculate the number of cells that will be in the contingency table. For example, if you want to construct a contingency table that would look at the five different categories of libraries in GROUP by four different benefit packages, you will have a contingency table with 20 cells (5 × 4 = 20). Therefore, you will need 20 columns in which to accumulate the totals.

On many spreadsheet programs with a fixed maximum size, this will limit the number of rows you can use for data entry. In these cases, you will have to save the interim results, as you did in the FREQ model.

CONTIN is also an example of use of the AND statement that is available on spreadsheet programs. It compares two different cells, and if they agree, a 1 is placed in the cell. If they disagree, a zero is placed in that cell. OR statements and NOT statements are similar to AND statements, and although they are not illustrated in this book, the CONTIN spreadsheet should give you a general idea of how they work.

The AND statement in cell C10 is

$$AND(A10=1,B10=1)$$

This can be read as Compare A10 and B10, and if they both are 1, place a 1 in cell C10. If they are not the same, place a zero in cell C10. Looking at the example spreadsheet, we see that the first entry is 2 for gender and 2 for use. Thus cell C10 is coded zero.

In rows 25 through 29 we are merely taking the summary information in row 23 and placing it in contingency table format.

Text and Formula Entry (See figure 44, Formula Worksheet)
Column A; Width = 10, Text Left for Rows 1 through 7
  Enter the text as given on the formula worksheet.
Columns B through H; Width = 10, Text Right
  Enter the text in B27 through B29.
  Enter the AND formulas in cells C10 through H10.
  REPLICATE each AND formula from row 10 to rows 11 through 21.
  Enter the SUM formula in cell C23 and REPLICATE it to cells D23 through H23.
  Enter the cell references in cells C27 through D29.

Using the Model
Enter the data in columns A and B for each case you are analyzing. You will not have enough rows for data entry (in most cases) and thus should expand the data-entry portion of the spreadsheet. Suggestions for expanding the spreadsheet are given in the discussion of FREQ.

XTAB: A Model for Cross-Tabulation and Calculation of Chi Square

Raw data can be converted into categorical data using GROUP, and two sets of grouped data can be combined through the use of CONTIN. XTAB provides a more detailed report than CONTIN because it calculates percentages, allowing comparison of cells. In addition, it provides the chi-square statistic, which describes the association between the two variables under study.

Three different types of percentaging are provided in XTAB (figure 45). "Row %" is the percentage of men and women of the total. "Column %" is the percentage of heavy, medium, and light use of "Total Use." "Cell %" is the percentage each individual cell represents of the total. (The general approach to the calculation of the chi-square statistic is taken from Blalock, pp. 211–21.)

General Design Features
There are three sections to the XTAB spreadsheet. The first is the data-entry portion in rows 9 through 11. Having this simple contingency table for data entry eases entering values in the report portion. The second, the report portion, accesses the data-entry table and computes the percentages and totals. The third calculates the chi-square statistic and the degrees of freedom.

	A	B	C	D	E	F	G	H
			CONTIN					
1	Filename:							
2	Date Created:							
3	Date Last Changed:							
4	=======	=======	=======	=======	=======	=======	=======	=======
5	CONTINGENCY TABLE CONSTRUCTION TEMPLATE							
6	Matches two sets of coded values for a two by three table							
7								
8	Gender	Use	Cell A	Cell B	Cell C	Cell D	Cell E	Cell F
9								
10	2	2	AND(A10=1,B10=1)	AND(A10=2,B10=1)	AND(A10=1,B10=2)	AND(A10=2,B10=2)	AND(A10=1,B10=3)	AND(A10=2,B10=3)
11	1	3	AND(A11=1,B11=1)	AND(A11=2,B11=1)	AND(A11=1,B11=2)	AND(A11=2,B11=2)	AND(A11=1,B11=3)	AND(A11=2,B11=3)
12	1	1	AND(A12=1,B12=1)	AND(A12=2,B12=1)	AND(A12=1,B12=2)	AND(A12=2,B12=2)	AND(A12=1,B12=3)	AND(A12=2,B12=3)
13	2	1	AND(A13=1,B13=1)	AND(A13=2,B13=1)	AND(A13=1,B13=2)	AND(A13=2,B13=2)	AND(A13=1,B13=3)	AND(A13=2,B13=3)
14	1	2	AND(A14=1,B14=1)	AND(A14=2,B14=1)	AND(A14=1,B14=2)	AND(A14=2,B14=2)	AND(A14=1,B14=3)	AND(A14=2,B14=3)
15	1	1	AND(A15=1,B15=1)	AND(A15=2,B15=1)	AND(A15=1,B15=2)	AND(A15=2,B15=2)	AND(A15=1,B15=3)	AND(A15=2,B15=3)
16	2	3	AND(A16=1,B16=1)	AND(A16=2,B16=1)	AND(A16=1,B16=2)	AND(A16=2,B16=2)	AND(A16=1,B16=3)	AND(A16=2,B16=3)
17	1	1	AND(A17=1,B17=1)	AND(A17=2,B17=1)	AND(A17=1,B17=2)	AND(A17=2,B17=2)	AND(A17=1,B17=3)	AND(A17=2,B17=3)
18	1	1	AND(A18=1,B18=1)	AND(A18=2,B18=1)	AND(A18=1,B18=2)	AND(A18=2,B18=2)	AND(A18=1,B18=3)	AND(A18=2,B18=3)
19	2	3	AND(A19=1,B19=1)	AND(A19=2,B19=1)	AND(A19=1,B19=2)	AND(A19=2,B19=2)	AND(A19=1,B19=3)	AND(A19=2,B19=3)
20	2	1	AND(A20=1,B20=1)	AND(A20=2,B20=1)	AND(A20=1,B20=2)	AND(A20=2,B20=2)	AND(A20=1,B20=3)	AND(A20=2,B20=3)
21	1	3	AND(A21=1,B21=1)	AND(A21=2,B21=1)	AND(A21=1,B21=2)	AND(A21=2,B21=2)	AND(A21=1,B21=3)	AND(A21=2,B21=3)
22			=========	=========	=========	=========	=========	=========
23			SUM(C10:C21)	SUM(D10:D21)	SUM(E10:E21)	SUM(F10:F21)	SUM(G10:G21)	SUM(H10:H21)
24								
25			WOMEN			MEN		
26								
27	HEAVY USE		C23			D23		
28	MEDIUM USE		E23			F23		
29	LIGHT USE		G23			H23		

Figure 44. CONTIN: Model for Constructing Contingency Tables, Formula Worksheet

```
   !  A  !!    B    !!    C    !!    D    !!    E    !!    F    !
 1 ! Filename:                    XTAB
 2 ! Date Created:
 3 ! Date Last Changed:
 4 ! ================================================================
 5 ! CROSSTABULATION AND CHI-SQUARE TEMPLATE
 6 ! Enter values in C9 through D11
 7 ! - - - - - - - - - - - - - - - - - - - - - - - - - - - - - - -
 8 !                            WOMEN        MEN
 9 !               HEAVY          12          36
10 !               MEDIUM         33          40
11 !               LIGHT         110         185
12 !
13 ! - - - - - - - - - - - - - - - - - - - - - - - - - - - - - -
14 !                                              GENDER
15 !
16 !                                   WOMEN         MEN        TOTAL
17 !
18 !    HEAVY      N                     12          36          48
19 !    USE        Row %              25.00       75.00      100.00
20 !               Column %            7.74       13.79       11.54
21 !               Cell %              2.88        8.65
22 !
23 !    MEDIUM     N                     33          40          73
24 !    USE        Row %              45.21       54.79      100.00
25 !               Column %           21.29       15.33       17.55
26 !               Cell %              7.93        9.62
27 !
28 !    LIGHT      N                    110         185         295
29 !    USE        Row %              37.29       62.71      100.00
30 !               Column %           70.97       70.88       70.91
31 !               Cell %             26.44       44.47
32 !
33 !                      ------------------------------------
34 !
35 !    TOTAL      N                    155         261         416
36 !               Row %              37.26       62.74      100.00
37 !               Column %          100.00      100.00      100.00
38 !
39 ! - - - - - - - - - - - - - - - - - - - - - - - - - - - - - - -
40 ! Statistical Analysis - Chi-square Statistic
41 !
42 !    Cell           Fo           Fe           Fo^2        Fo^2/Fe
43 !
44 !    A              12     17.88461538462      144     8.051612903226
45 !    B              36     30.11538461538     1296    43.03448275862
46 !    C              33     27.19951923077     1089    40.03747238179
47 !    D              40     45.80048076923     1600    34.93413110796
48 !    E             110    109.9158653846     12100   110.0841990159
49 !    F             185    185.0841346154     34225   184.9159036301
50 !
51 ! Total           416            416                  421.0578017976
52 !
53 !        Chi-square =      5.057801797564
54 !        # Rows =                       3
55 !        # Columns =                    2
56 !        df =                           2
```

Figure 45. XTAB: Cross-Tabulation and Chi Square Model, Example Spreadsheet

The references to the "cells" A through F in A44 through A49 follow this pattern.

	Women	*Men*
Heavy	A	B
Medium	C	D
Light	E	F

If you wish to modify this spreadsheet to include various contingency table sizes (2 by 2, 3 by 4, etc.), you should follow the convention of lettering the table cells, starting at the upper left and proceeding across the columns, then to the next row, far left to the right, and so on. Thus a four-by-four table would appear as follows:

A	B	C	D
E	F	G	H
I	J	K	L
M	N	O	P

In calculating the chi-square statistic, you must find the *Fe* (frequency of the expected) by multiplying the right total by the bottom total and dividing by the total-total. Look at the first Fe formula in cell C44 to see how this is done. The remainder of the calculation of the chi-square statistic involves squaring the *Fo* (frequency of the observed) and dividing that number by the Fe value. These are summed and the Fo sum is subtracted from the Fo^2/Fe sum.

Rather than revise the spreadsheet each time you have a different-size contingency table, I suggest that you prepare a series of models for each of the most useful contingency table sizes. For most contingency problems you will not exceed a five-by-five table. Thus you might design models for the following table sizes:

2 by 2	2 by 3	2 by 4	2 by 5
3 by 3	3 by 4	3 by 5	
4 by 4	4 by 5	5 by 5	

You should be able to place several of the smaller models on one spreadsheet file. Also, if you are not interested in the percentaging, eliminate all the rows that contain percents. This will decrease the size of your model considerably.

Text and Formula Entry (See figure 46, Formula Worksheet)

The time-saving techniques of replication, copying, and so forth are not useful in designing this model. For the most part, you will have to enter each formula individually. You may REPLICATE the formulas in rows 44 through 49 (columns C through E), but the rest of the spreadsheet cannot use that feature efficiently.

In general, all text is right justified (Text Right), and the columns are formated to a width of 15. If you can format blocks of cells, round off the percentage cells to two decimal places.

Using the Model

Enter the data in cells C9 through D11. Calculation takes place automatically.

Find the table (usually an appendix in most statistics texts) for the distribution of chi square to find the significance level of the chi square you have computed for the degrees of freedom in your table.

```
  !  A   !!    B      !!    C     !!    D     !!    E     !!    F     !
 1 ! Filename:                     XTAB
 2 ! Date Created:
 3 ! Date Last Changed:
 4 ! ================================================================
 5 ! CROSSTABULATION AND CHI-SQUARE TEMPLATE
 6 ! Enter values in C9 through D11
 7 ! - - - - - - - - - - - - - - - - - - - - - - - - - - - - - - - -
 8 !                            WOMEN        MEN
 9 !             HEAVY            12          36
10 !             MEDIUM           33          40
11 !             LIGHT           110         185
12 !
13 ! - - - - - - - - - - - - - - - - - - - - - - - - - - - - - - - -
14 !                                                GENDER
15 !
16 !                                 WOMEN           MEN          TOTAL
17 !
18 !   HEAVY      N                    C9             D9         D18+E18
19 !   USE        Row %          D18/F18 * 100  E18/F18 * 100  F18/F18 * 100
20 !              Column %       D18/D35 * 100  E18/E35 * 100  F18/F35 * 100
21 !              Cell %         D18/F35 * 100  E18/F35 * 100
22 !
23 !   MEDIUM     N                    C10            D10        D23+E23
24 !   USE        Row %          D23/F23 * 100  E23/F23 * 100  F23/F23 * 100
25 !              Column %       D23/D35 * 100  E23/E35 * 100  F23/F35 * 100
26 !              Cell %         D23/F35 * 100  E23/F35 * 100
27 !
28 !   LIGHT      N                    C11            D11        D28+E28
29 !   USE        Row %          D28/F28 * 100  E28/F28 * 100  F28/F28 * 100
30 !              Column %       D28/D35 * 100  E28/E35 * 100  F28/F35 * 100
31 !              Cell %         D28/F35 * 100  E28/F35 * 100
32 !
33 !                           -------------------------------------------
34 !
35 !   TOTAL      N            D18+D23+D28    E18+E23+E28    F18+F23+F28
36 !              Row %          D35/F35 * 100  E35/F35 * 100  F35/F35 * 100
37 !              Column %     D20+D25+D30    E20+E25+E30    F20+F25+F30
38 !
39 ! - - - - - - - - - - - - - - - - - - - - - - - - - - - - - - - -
40 ! Statistical Analysis - Chi-square Statistic
41 !
42 !    Cell           Fo             Fe            Fo^2         Fo^2/Fe
43 !
44 !     A            D18        (F18 * D35)/F35   B44 * B44    D44/C44
45 !     B            E18        (F18 * E35)/F35   B45 * B45    D45/C45
46 !     C            D23        (F23 * D35)/F35   B46 * B46    D46/C46
47 !     D            E23        (F23 * E35)/F35   B47 * B47    D47/C47
48 !     E            D28        (F28 * D35)/F35   B48 * B48    D48/C48
49 !     F            E28        (F28 * E35)/F35   B49 * B49    D49/C49
50 !
51 ! Total      SUM(B44:B49)    SUM(C44:C49)                 SUM(E44:E49)
52 !
53 !         Chi-square =    E51-B51
54 !         # Rows =        3
55 !         # Columns =     2
56 !         df =            (C54-1) * (C55-1)
```

Figure 46. XTAB: Cross-Tabulation and Chi Square Model, Formula Worksheet

LQ: A Model to Compare Libraries Using O'Connor's Library Quotient

Comparing libraries appears to be a common pastime in librarianship, especially during budget preparation time. While the recent history of public library administration stresses the development of local goals, objectives, and plans, the practice of comparing library A with "similar" libraries persists. In the academic library field, comparisons are also present, as in the annual report on ARL statistics. While a sophisticated regression model has been constructed to analyze ARL statistics, its computational requirements are probably too sophisticated for many librarians.

Daniel O. O'Connor's *Library Quotient* (or LQ)[1] is a method of comparison that should be familiar to most people. It is the well-known IQ score (or Intelligence Quotient) adapted for libraries. Using this method, a score of 100 is "average"; anything exceeding a score of 115 is significantly higher than average while anything lower than 85 is significantly lower than average. Thus libraries can compare their resources, or outputs, with other libraries and have a measure of "significant departure" from the average.

O'Connor's LQ can be used with resource measures (titles held or added, funds expended, staff employed, etc.) or output measures (circulation, reference activity, document delivery capability, etc.). While public libraries are used as examples by O'Connor, academic and school libraries can use the techniques as well.

The statistics used for comparison must be in ratio form. The most common ratio measure is the per capita measure or the per student measure. You can also use such ratio measures as "per dollar of expenditure" or "per item circulated."

Figure 47. LQ: Model to Compare Libraries, Example Spreadsheet

	A	B	C	D	E	F
1	Filename:		LQ			
2	Date Created:					
3	Date Last Changed:					
4	===					
5	LIBRARY QUOTIENT CALCULATOR					
6	See Daniel O. O'Connor, "Evaluating Public Libraries Using Standard					
7	Scores: The Library Quotient", Library Research 4, 51-70 (1982).					
8	---					
9	Enter ratio data (e.g., Circulation Per Capita) in Column B					
10	---					
11	Library	Circ	X^2	Stan.		LQ
12	Number	Per Capita		Score		
13	- -					
14	1	.51	.2601	-1.43099495		79
15	2	1.76	3.0976	-1.15375632		83
16	3	6.63	43.9569	-.073634582		99
17	4	2.82	7.9524	-.918657951		86
18	5	6.87	47.1969	-.020404764		100
19	6	9.72	94.4784	.6116993313		109
20	7	6.96	48.4416	-.000443582		100
21	8	5.72	32.7184	-.275464311		96
22	9	14.46	209.0916	1.662988247		125
23	10	14.17	200.7889	1.598668883		124
24	- -					
25	Sum Ratios					69.62
26	Mean ratios					6.962
27	N Ratios					10
28	Sum X^2					687.9828
29	Stan. Dev					4.508751047

1. Daniel O. O'Connor, "Evaluating Public Libraries Using Standard Scores: The Library Quotient," *Library Research*, 4:51–70 (1982).

General Design Features

The example model (figure 47) is limited to a total of ten libraries. This model can easily be expanded to include substantially larger numbers of libraries. Thus state library agencies could use the model to study large groups of libraries within the state as well. Limits on the size of the spreadsheet are imposed by the capacity of your spreadsheet program.

The ratio score is entered in column B, rows 14 through 23. This score is then squared in column C. The standard score is computed in column D, based on the average and standard deviation of all the scores, and is converted into the LQ score in column E.

Most of the formula entry can be performed by using the REPLICATE function of spreadsheet programs. The formula for the standard deviation is the same as that used in DSTAT and CORREG.

Text and Formula Entry (See figure 48, Formula Worksheet)

Column A; Width = 12, Text Left

Enter the text in column A. Use the REPEAT ENTRY function to enter the long lines where indicated.

Columns B through E; Width = 12, Text Right

Enter the headings in rows 11 and 12.

Column B

This column is used for data entry.

Column C

Square the number in column B. Enter the formula in cell C14 and REPLICATE it to C15 through C23.

Enter the formulas in C25 through C29. If you are expanding the spreadsheet to include more libraries, make sure the final reference (now C23) reflects this new range.

	A	B	C	D	E	F
1	Filename:		LQ			
2	Date Created:					
3	Date Last Changed:					
4	==					
5	LIBRARY QUOTIENT CALCULATOR					
6	See Daniel O. O'Connor, "Evaluating Public Libraries Using Standard					
7	Scores: The Library Quotient", Library Research 4, 51-70 (1982).					
8	---					
9	Enter ratio data (e.g., Circulation Per Capita) in Column B					
10	---					
11	Library	Circ	X^2	Stan.	LQ	
12	Number	Per Capita		Score		
13	- -					
14	1	.51	B14*B14	(B14-C26)/C29	15*D14+100	
15	2	1.76	B15*B15	(B15-C26)/C29	15*D15+100	
16	3	6.63	B16*B16	(B16-C26)/C29	15*D16+100	
17	4	2.82	B17*B17	(B17-C26)/C29	15*D17+100	
18	5	6.87	B18*B18	(B18-C26)/C29	15*D18+100	
19	6	9.72	B19*B19	(B19-C26)/C29	15*D19+100	
20	7	6.96	B20*B20	(B20-C26)/C29	15*D20+100	
21	8	5.72	B21*B21	(B21-C26)/C29	15*D21+100	
22	9	14.46	B22*B22	(B22-C26)/C29	15*D22+100	
23	10	14.17	B23*B23	(B23-C26)/C29	15*D23+100	
24	- -					
25	Sum Ratios		SUM(B14:B23)			
26	Mean ratios		AVERAGE(B14:B23)			
27	N Ratios		COUNT(B14:B23)			
28	Sum X^2		SUM(C14:C23)			
29	Stan. Dev		(1/C27)*SQRT((C27*C28)-(C25*C25))			

Figure 48. LQ: Model to Compare Libraries, Formula Worksheet

Column D
> Enter the formula in D14 to compute the standard score. REPLICATE this formula to D15 through D23, but make sure that the references to C26 and C29 *do not change*.

Column E
> Enter the LQ formula in cell E14. REPLICATE the formula to E15 through E23.

Using the Model

Enter the ratio scores in column B. You will find that you have to "recalculate" this model at least once. Usually this is done by entering an exclamation point.

You can copy the entire data entry and calculation portion several times to other areas of the spreadsheet so that you can enter several different comparative measures. If you wish, you can then find the "average LQ" on all the measures for an overall LQ score.

SSIZE: A Model for Calculating Sample Size

The question I have been asked most frequently in my role as teacher and research advisor has been "What size of a sample do I need?" The answer involves asking a number of other and different questions. The response is usually "It all depends."

The most common method for determining sample size is the one given in the illustration. It assumes that the data will be continuous (at the ratio scale level) and that you have decided upon three key factors:

1. You know the confidence level you want to achieve.
2. You know how accurate you want to be (this is termed *tolerance*).
3. You have some estimate of the standard deviation of the variable that is most important in your study.

Typically, the confidence level is set at 95 or 99 percent for most problems. The tolerance must be based on your knowledge of the problem and your requirements for accuracy. If your tolerance is set at 2, as in the example, you will be able to say that you can estimate the mean from the sample within plus or minus 2 units of measurement. Finally, you need to estimate the standard deviation you might tentatively compute with a very small "sample" using the CORREG spreadsheet.

SSIZE asks you to enter these three factors. The sample size is then computed. For purposes of illustrating the use of the LOOKUP function, all the z-scores associated with the confidence levels from 90 to 99 percent are included. A caution is in order here. Choosing a confidence level of 98 percent (as in the example) may give a spurious

Figure 49. SSIZE: Sample Size Calculator, Example Spreadsheet

	A	B	C	D	E	F	G
1	Filename:		SSIZE				
2	Date Created:						
3	Date Last Changed:						
4	==						
5	SAMPLE SIZE CALCULATOR						
6	--						
7	Enter the following in A8 through A10:					LOOKUP TABLE	
8	98		Confidence Level (90% through 99%)			90	1.65
9	2		Desired Tolerance			91	1.69
10	15		Estimated Standard Deviation			92	1.75
11	---					93	1.81
12	SAMPLE SIZE =	305				94	1.88
13						95	1.96
14						96	2.05
15						97	2.17
16						98	2.33
17						99	2.58

```
     !    A    !!   B   !!   C   !!   D   !!   E   !!   F   !!   G   !
 1 ! Filename:              SSIZE
 2 ! Date Created:
 3 ! Date Last Changed:
 4 ! =================================================
 5 ! SAMPLE SIZE CALCULATOR
 6 ! -------------------------------------------------
 7 ! Enter the following in A8 through A10:           LOOKUP TABLE
 8 ! 98            Confidence Level (90% through 99%)     90      1.65
 9 ! 2             Desired Tolerance                      91      1.69
10 ! 15            Estimated Standard Deviation           92      1.75
11 ! ----------------------------------------            93      1.81
12 ! SAMPLE SIZE =   (((LOOKUP(A8,F8:F17) * A10)/A9)^2)   94      1.88
13 !                                                      95      1.96
14 !                                                      96      2.05
15 !                                                      97      2.17
16 !                                                      98      2.33
17 !                                                      99      2.58
```

Figure 50. SSIZE:
Sample Size Calculator,
Formula Worksheet

impression of accuracy. It is best to stick with the conventional use of the 95 and 99 percent levels.

Another method of determining sample size that is less well known is the subject of a paper I published in *Library and Information Science Research* (Winter 1984), entitled "Sample Size Determination: A Comparison of Attribute, Continuous Variable, and Cell Size Methods." This is what I term the *cell-size method*. Without a long explanation of the rationale behind the process, you can use the CONTIN spreadsheet concept to determine sample size using this method.

In the cell-size method, you must figure out the most complex interrelationship of variables you will simultaneously analyze in your final report. If you are constructing a four-by-four table and this is the largest you will use in your analysis, you multiply the number of cells in that table by 20 to arrive at the sample size. Therefore, a four-by-four table yields 16 cells. The number of cells is multiplied by a factor of 20, to arrive at a sample size of 320. If three variables are involved and the third one is a variable with (for example) three categories, your final table would have 48 cells ($4 \times 4 \times 3 = 48$), and multiplying by 20 would yield a sample size of 960.

The example given here is for continuous data and is the most widely accepted approach to calculating sample size (figure 49).

General Design Features

The SSIZE spreadsheet involves only one formula and a reference to a LOOKUP table. Data entry takes place in cells A8 through A10, and the result is presented in B12.

You can use the model to see what combinations of confidence level and tolerance lead to the lowest acceptable sample size.

Text and Formula Entry (See figure 50, Formula Worksheet)

Column A

Enter the text as given. In using the model, you must decide on the confidence level, tolerance, and standard deviation you wish to enter. Enter the long lines as "repeat entries".

Column B

Enter the text in rows 8 through 10.
Enter the formula as given in cell B12.

Column F

Enter the confidence levels 90 through 99 in rows 8 through 17.

Column G

Enter the associated z-scores in rows 8 through 17.

Accessing Data from Different
Spreadsheet Models

The spreadsheet models that have been presented in this book contain data that can be used to complete surveys and questionnaires you receive from outside agencies. Most public librarians must complete an annual report for their State Library that typically asks for information on income and expenditures, staffing levels, collection size, and circulation output. Academic librarians may have to complete the Higher Education General Information Survey (HEGIS) every two years, or if they are members of ARL, complete the annual report form. Local governing bodies, state and national associations, and the occasional researcher may request quantitative information on your library's resources and performance.

This book does not contain a complete system of statistical reporting for each type of library. The models that are presented must be modified to include information that has relevance to your operations and to your reporting needs. It is hoped that you will develop a full-fledged statistical reporting system using your spreadsheet program. In designing that system, take into account the regular reports you will have to prepare for these external agencies.

The following spreadsheets are not so much calculating models as reporting models. The spreadsheets HEGIS, PLSTAT, and ARLSTAT are literal copies of recently used reporting forms. They are designed to allow you to keep a record of which *other* spreadsheets contain the data you must report.

In transferring the data from the other spreadsheets to these reporting spreadsheets, it is often easiest to do the transfer manually. That is, find the needed piece of information and retype it into the reporting spreadsheet. Integrated software, such as Lotus' "Symphony," Ashton-Tate's "Framework," and Apple's Lisa and MacIntosh hardware/software combination, will assist you a great deal in this assembling process.

HEGIS: The Higher Education General Information Survey

The biannual Higher Education General Information Survey, better known as the HEGIS Survey, is familiar to many college and university librarians. Its companion survey, the Library General Information (or LIBGIS) Survey, seeks similar information from the public library community. Many of the items overlap both surveys, and in the example spreadsheet (figure 51), these overlaps are noted by core numbers which are displayed in column H.

The HEGIS and LIBGIS surveys are really reports. Only a small amount of calculation takes place in the report itself. The data that are requested will be on other spreadsheet models that you have prepared, such as ACTIVCL or DISBYR. Unless you are using spreadsheet programs with virtual memory or "integrated software," you will find it easiest to transfer the requested information manually to the HEGIS model.

General Design Features

The HEGIS form has been copied onto a spreadsheet that is called HEGIS. Columns A and B are used to refer to other spreadsheets, from which data will be carried, by filename and cell number.

By listing the filenames and locations for each requested data element, you will be able to determine which pieces of data you have and which you do not have. The example spreadsheets in this book do not contain all the requested data, and therefore you will have to modify several spreadsheets or design new ones to collect the requested data.

One part of the HEGIS report that requires a sizable bit of calculating is part 2, section A, where details on staffing, annual salaries, and wages are requested for four groups of employees and, within each group, for men and women. The next spreadsheet, HEGISAID, is designed to calculate your personnel data according to the directions supplied with the HEGIS form.

In columns G and H, the terms *Line No.* and *Core No.* have no meaning for you. They are used by the HEGIS staff to enter the responses into proper locations for their computer processing. They are reproduced here only because they were on the HEGIS survey instrument.

Text Entry

Columns A and B are used to record where the requested information is located in your other spreadsheet models. Columns C through H indicate the required data and the location on the HEGIS report form where the data are to be entered. In general, columns I and J are used to enter the data you obtain from your other spreadsheets.

Using the Model

If you wish, you can record a series of years of this type of data by creating "year" columns to the right of the present data. Thus you could record the 1984, 1986, 1988 (and on) data on the same spreadsheet. Analysis of the trends in these data can be performed by using the CORREG spreadsheet model.

HEGISAID: A Calculation Model to Prepare Salary and Wage Data for Entry into the HEGIS Report

The spreadsheet HEGISAID is designed to prepare the data required in part 2, section 5 of the HEGIS report. This section requires you to enter the number of persons, full time and part time, who worked in your library during the reporting year; the full-time equivalency of part-time workers; and the annual salaries paid to each staff member. For calculation of the Corrected Annual Salary, 10-month salaries must be adjusted to the equivalent 12-month salary. The form used in this example was dated 1982 and should be reviewed for possible changes in later years.

Four major categories of personnel are listed on the HEGIS report. For each category, data are requested for both men and women. Therefore, eight different computations must be made in order to complete the report.

General Design Features

The HEGISAID spreadsheet is divided into two parts (figure 52). The upper part is the actual calculation model. The lower part is for storing the results of each of the eight computations you must make.

	A	B	C	D	F	G	H	I	J	K
1	Filename:									
2	Date Created:									
3	Date Last Changed:									
6	FILENAME	LOCATION	HEGIS	Description						
8				Part I – Periodicals and Library Collections						
10				Section A – Current Periodical Subscriptions		LINE NO.	CORE NO.			
12	ACTIVCL	L49		CURRENT PERIODICAL SUBSCRIPTIONS		1	20			
14				Section B – Library Collection				ADDED DURING YEAR	HELD AT END OF YEAR	
16				Bookstock						
17	ACTIVCL	L45		NUMBER OF VOLUMES		2	16			
18	ACTIVCL			NUMBER OF TITLES		3	17			
19				Separate Government Documents Collections						
20	ACTIVCL	L46		NUMBER OF VOLUMES		4				
21				Microforms – All Types						
22	ACTIVCL			NUMBER OF BOOK TITLES		5	21			
23	ACTIVCL			NUMBER OF PERIODICAL TITLES		6	22			
24	ACTIVCL			NUMBER NOT REPORTED IN LINES 5 AND 6		7	23			
25				Audiovisual Materials						
26	ACTIVCL			NUMBER OF TITLES		8	24			
27	ACTIVCL			ALL OTHER LIBRARY MATERIALS		9	25			
29				Part II – Library Staff						
31				Section A – Library Staffing and Annual Salaries and Wages						
33				POSITION	SEX	LINE NO.	FULL TIME NUMBER OF PERSONS	PART TIME NUMBER OF PERSONS	FULL TIME EQUIVALENCY	ANNUAL SALARIES FULL TIME (as corrected)
36	HEGISAID			CHIEF, DEPUTY, ASSOCIATE AND	MEN	10	2	1	.43	$106,901
37	HEGISAID			ASSISTANT CHIEF LIBRARIANS	WOMEN	11	3	2	1.14	$115,936
39	HEGISAID			ALL OTHER LIBRARIANS	MEN	12	2	2	1.37	$70,221
40	HEGISAID				WOMEN	13	7	5	2.37	$185,676
42	HEGISAID			OTHER PROFESSIONAL STAFF ON	MEN	14				
43	HEGISAID			THE LIBRARY BUDGET	WOMEN	15				
45	HEGISAID			TECHNICAL AND CLERICAL STAFF	MEN	16				
46	HEGISAID			ON THE LIBRARY BUDGET	WOMEN	17				
48	HEGISAID			TOTAL (Sum of lines 10 through 17)		18	14	10	5.31	$478,734
50				Section B – Number of Hours of Student Assistance						
52				Number of Hours of Student Assistance by		LINE NO.		NUMBER OF HOURS		
53				Students Employed on an Hourly Basis						
55	STDEMP			HOURS CHARGED TO LIBRARY BUDGET		19				
56	STDEMP			HOURS CHARGED TO BUDGETS OTHER THAN THE LIBRARY		20				

Row	A	B	C	G	H	I
57						
58			Part III – Developmental Areas			
59			Section A – Library Loan Transactions			
60						
61				LINE NO.	CORE NO.	NUMBER
62	ACTIVCL	M25	CIRCULATION OF MATERIALS TO LIBRARY USERS	21	26	
63			Interlibrary Loans			
64	ACTIVCL	M34	PROVIDED TO OTHER LIBRARIES	22	27	
65	ACTIVCL	M35	RECEIVED FROM OTHER LIBRARIES	23	28	
66						
67			Section B – Transactions			
68						NUMBER
69	ACTIVCL	M38	TOTAL REFERENCE TRANSACTIONS	24	35	
70	ACTIVCL		TOTAL GROUP TRANSACTIONS	25		
71	ACTIVCL		TOTAL PERSONS PARTICIPATING IN GROUP TRANSACTIONS	26		
72						
73			Section C – Library Hours and Days Open Per Week			NUMBER
74						
75	ACTIVCL		TOTAL HOURS OPEN PER TYPICAL WEEK	27	32	
76	ACTIVCL		TOTAL DAYS OPEN TWO HOURS OR MORE, TYPICAL WEEK	28	33	
77						
78			Part IV – Library Finances	LINE NO.	CORE NO.	EXPENDITURES
79			Section A – Library Operating Expenditures			
80						
81						
82			Salaries and Wages			
83	DISBYR		SALARIES AND WAGES OF LIBRARY STAFF	29	5	
84	DISBYR		FRINGE BENEFITS	30		
85	DISBYR		WAGES OF STUDENTS SERVING ON AN HOURLY BASIS	31		
86			Materials			
87	DISBYR		BOOKS	32	6	
88	DISBYR		PERIODICALS	33	7	
89	DISBYR		MICROFORMS	34	8	
90	DISBYR		AUDIOVISUAL MATERIALS	35		
91	DISBYR		ALL OTHER LIBRARY MATERIALS	36	9	
92	DISBYR		BINDING AND REBINDING	37	11	
93	DISBYR		ALL OTHER LIBRARY OPERATING EXPENDITURES	38	14	
94	DISBYR		TOTAL LIBRARY OPERATING EXPENDITURES	39	15	
95						
96			Section B – Library Receipts from Federal Grants			RECEIPTS
97						
98	DISBYR		TOTAL RECEIPTS FROM FEDERAL GRANTS	40		

Figure 51. HEGIS: Higher Education General Information Survey Report, Example Spreadsheet

	A	B	C	D	E	F	G	H	I	J	K	L
1	Filename:											
2	Date Created:											
3	Date Last Changed:											
4												
5	HEGIS LIBRARY STAFF CALCULATION AID AND REPORT GENERATOR											

Hours in Work Week: 35

Line	EMPLOYEE NAME	10 MO. APPT.	12 MO. APPT.	FULL TIME	PART TIME	IF PART TIME, HRS PER WEEK	PART TIME FTE	ANNUAL SALARY	CORRECTED ANN. SAL.
10	Emily		1	1			.00	$18,975	$18,975
11	Barbara	1		1			.00	$18,975	$23,192
12	Elaine				1	20	.57	$18,975	$10,843
13	Joyce	1			1	10	.29	$15,000	$4,286
14	Ellen		1	1			.00	$15,000	$18,333
15	Mildred		1	1			.00	$15,000	$15,000
16	Susan				1	20	.57	$21,000	$12,000
17	Lynn			1			.00	$21,000	$25,667
18	Kathy	1		1			.00	$21,000	$25,667
19	Priscilla	1		1			.43	$15,000	$6,429
20	Jill				1	15	.51	$20,000	$10,286
21	Jennifer				1	18			
22									
23	TOTALS	4	3	7	5		2.37	$214,925	$185,676

HEGIS REPORT SECTION

POSITION	SEX	LINE NO.	FULL TIME NUMBER OF PERSONS	PART TIME NUMBER OF PERSONS	PART TIME FULL TIME EQUIVALENCY	ANNUAL SALARIES FULL TIME (as corrected)
CHIEF, DEPUTY, ASSOCIATE AND	MEN	10	2	1	.43	$106,901
ASSISTANT CHIEF LIBRARIANS	WOMEN	11	3	2	1.14	$115,936
ALL OTHER LIBRARIANS	MEN	12	2	2	1.37	$70,221
	WOMEN	13	7	5	2.37	$185,676
OTHER PROFESSIONAL STAFF ON	MEN	14				
THE LIBRARY BUDGET	WOMEN	15				
TECHNICAL AND CLERICAL STAFF	MEN	16				
ON THE LIBRARY BUDGET	WOMEN	17				
TOTAL (Sum of lines 10 through 17)		18	14	10	5.31	$478,734

Figure 52. HEGISAID: Calculation Model for HEGIS Data, Example Spreadsheet

I have provided space for twelve employees to be listed. (You may have to expand the spreadsheet if you have more than twelve employees in a given gender/position classification.) For each employee, you enter the type of appointment (10 or 12 months) if they are full-time staff. If they are part-time staff, you should not enter anything in the columns for 10- and 12-month appointments. Indicate whether the person is a full- or part-time staff member in columns G and H. For part-time staff, enter the usual number of hours worked per week. The spreadsheet will then calculate the Part-Time FTE. Finally, enter the Annual Salary for each employee in column K. The Corrected Annual Salary is then computed according to the instructions supplied on the HEGIS form.

After you have entered all persons for a particular position classification and gender, the totals appear in row 23. Transfer the four required pieces of information from cells G23, H23, J23, and L23 to the report section at the bottom of the spreadsheet. This transfer could be accomplished by a series of IF statements, but it is easier just to type in the numbers.

The nested IF statement in cell L10 is

$$IF(E10=1,K10*1.22222,IF(H10=1,J10*K10,K10))$$

This formula does the following. First it checks to see IF there is a number 1 in cell E10, which indicates that this person has a 10-month appointment. IF there is a 1 in E10, it multiplies the annual salary by 1.22222 (or 11/9ths) to make it equivalent to a 12-month appointment. Next, IF the part-time cell (H10) has a 1, it multiplies the FTE factor by the annual salary to come up with an equivalent salary for 12 months. Finally, IF neither the 10-month cell is checked nor the part-time cell, the formula assumes this was a 12-month appointment and enters the annual salary found in K10.

All relevant columns are then summed in row 23.

In the example, the results of this particular computation are entered into row 35, which reports on All Other Librarians–Women.

Notice that the formulas in column J reference the normal hours in a work week figure that you enter in cell H5. If different classes of staff have different work weeks, this figure should be changed accordingly.

Text and Formula Entry (See figure 53, Formula Worksheet)

Columns A through D; Width = 20, Text Left
There are no formulas or numbers in these columns. Enter the text as given.

Columns E through L; Width = 20, Text Right
Enter the headings for the columns in rows 7, 8, 27, 28, and 29.

Column E
Enter the SUM formula in cell E23. REPLICATE E23 to F23 through L23. Go back to cell I23 and DELETE that formula. It is not needed.

Column J
Enter the division formula in cell J10. REPLICATE J10 to J11 through J21, making sure that the reference to H5 in the formula *does not change*.

Column L
Enter the IF formula in cell L10. REPLICATE L10 to L11 through L21. All the cell references are "relative" in this formula (i.e., they *do* change).

96

HEGIS LIBRARY STAFF CALCULATION AID AND REPORT GENERATOR

Hours in Work Week: 35

Row	EMPLOYEE NAME	10 MO. APPT.	12 MO. APPT.	FULL TIME	PART TIME	IF PART TIME, HRS PER WEEK	PART TIME FTE	ANNUAL SALARY	CORRECTED ANN. SAL.
10	Emily		1	1			I10/H5	18975	IF(E10=1,K10*1.22222,IF(H10=1,J10*K10,K10))
11	Barbara	1		1			I11/H5	18975	IF(E11=1,K11*1.22222,IF(H11=1,J11*K11,K11))
12	Elaine				1	20	I12/H5	18975	IF(E12=1,K12*1.22222,IF(H12=1,J12*K12,K12))
13	Joyce				1	10	I13/H5	15000	IF(E13=1,K13*1.22222,IF(H13=1,J13*K13,K13))
14	Ellen	1		1			I14/H5	15000	IF(E14=1,K14*1.22222,IF(H14=1,J14*K14,K14))
15	Mildred		1	1			I15/H5	15000	IF(E15=1,K15*1.22222,IF(H15=1,J15*K15,K15))
16	Susan		1	1			I16/H5	15000	IF(E16=1,K16*1.22222,IF(H16=1,J16*K16,K16))
17	Lynn				1	20	I17/H5	21000	IF(E17=1,K17*1.22222,IF(H17=1,J17*K17,K17))
18	Kathy	1		1			I18/H5	21000	IF(E18=1,K18*1.22222,IF(H18=1,J18*K18,K18))
19	Priscilla	1		1			I19/H5	21000	IF(E19=1,K19*1.22222,IF(H19=1,J19*K19,K19))
20	Jill				1	15	I20/H5	15000	IF(E20=1,K20*1.22222,IF(H20=1,J20*K20,K20))
21	Jennifer				1	18	I21/H5	20000	IF(E21=1,K21*1.22222,IF(H21=1,J21*K21,K21))
23	TOTALS	SUM(E10:E21)	SUM(F10:F21)	SUM(G10:G21)	SUM(H10:H21)		SUM(J10:J21)	SUM(K10:K21)	SUM(L10:L21)

HEGIS REPORT SECTION

Row	POSITION	SEX	LINE NO.	FULL TIME NUMBER OF PERSONS	PART TIME NUMBER OF PERSONS	PART TIME FULL TIME EQUIVALENCY	ANNUAL SALARIES FULL TIME (as corrected)
31	CHIEF, DEPUTY, ASSOCIATE AND	MEN	10	2	1	.43	106901
32	ASSISTANT CHIEF LIBRARIANS	WOMEN	11	3	2	1.14	115936
34	ALL OTHER LIBRARIANS	MEN	12	2	2	1.37	70221
35		WOMEN	13	7	5	2.37	185676
37	OTHER PROFESSIONAL STAFF ON	MEN	14				
38	THE LIBRARY BUDGET	WOMEN	15				
40	TECHNICAL AND CLERICAL STAFF	MEN	16				
41	ON THE LIBRARY BUDGET	WOMEN	17				
43	TOTAL (Sum of lines 10 through 17)		18	SUM(F31:F41)	SUM(G31:G41)	SUM(H31:H41)	SUM(I31:I41)

Figure 53. HEGISAID: Calculation Model for HEGIS Data, Formula Worksheet

Using the Model

After you have entered the data in columns E through I and K, transfer the results to the appropriate row in the report portion of the spreadsheet. When you have completed the report, transfer the figures to your HEGIS report.

Assembling public library statistics for a state library agency is done annually in most states. The forms vary considerably from state to state and the one used here may not be typical (figure 54). This form was used in New Jersey to report statistics for the year 1983 and contains data that are often requested in other states. Obviously, you must modify this spreadsheet to reflect your state's reporting format.

PLSTAT: A Model to Assemble and Calculate Data for a State Report on Public Library Statistics

General Design Features

The approach is the same as in the HEGIS spreadsheet. That is, space is provided in columns A and B to enter references to the filename and the location of the requested data. You will gather the data to complete the report from various files you have designed and assemble them here to complete the report. This is really a convenient listing of where data reside on your other files.

This book does not contain examples of all the data required to complete this form. You must design spreadsheets that record and summarize the data your state requires. If your reporting system does not contain categories asked for by the state agency, you should develop parallel files in the state agency format to ease preparation of the state's report.

In this example, the only procedure which is not covered elsewhere in the book is the formula below:

SUM(L35:M36)

This formula sums a range of values: L35 through M36. That is, four cells are summed: L35, L36, M35, and M36. If you have a large block of numbers that must be summed, using the range specification in this way results in a much shorter formula. However, not all spreadsheet programs allow you to sum this type of range. Try it. If it does not work, use the formula L35+L36+M35+M36.

Text and Formula Entry (See figure 55, Formula Worksheet)

Columns A through I; Width = 9, Text Left
> Taking into account the length of your text entries, set up as many columns as you need to contain the text. If you can format individual columns to a certain width, you will format column C to something like 50 characters.

Column J
> These line numbers are supplied on the New Jersey form and may not be provided by your state library agency.

Columns L and M
> Enter the formulas as given. There is little opportunity to use the replicating feature in this particular state report.

Text continues on page 106.

	A	B	C	D	E	F	G	H	I	J	K	L	M
1	Filename:	PLSTAT											
2	Date Created:												
3	Date Last Changed:												

PUBLIC LIBRARY STATISTICAL REPORT

FILENAME LOCATION YEAR:

PART 1: LIBRARY INCOME

	LINE NUMBER	AMOUNT
BALANCE BROUGHT FORWARD	11	$24,191
LOCAL TAX SUPPORT		
Municipal/County Appropriation	12	$474,400
Additional Tax Support	13	$121,729
TOTAL LOCAL TAX SUPPORT	14	$596,129
CONTRACTUAL	15	$0
STATE AID		
Per Capita	16	$35,490
Other	17	$500
TOTAL STATE AID	18	$35,990
FEDERAL		
LSCA	19	$0
Other	20	$0
Other	21	$0
TOTAL FEDERAL	22	$0
OTHER INCOME	23	$26,479
TOTAL INCOME	24	$682,789
CAPITAL BUDGET INCOME	25	$28,000

PART 2: LIBRARY OPERATING EXPENDITURES FROM ALL SOURCES

	LINE NUMBER	AMOUNT Local, Other Funds	AMOUNT Per Capita State Aid
SALARIES AND WAGES	26	$336,021	$33,721
FRINGE BENEFITS	27	$85,548	$0
TOTAL PERSONNEL – ALL SOURCES	28	$455,290	/////
MATERIALS			
BOOKS	29	$50,959	$0
PERIODICALS	30	$8,752	$0
AUDIOVISUAL MATERIALS	31	$3,603	$0
OTHER LIBRARY MATERIALS	32	$1,173	$0
TOTAL MATERIALS	33	$64,487	/////
ALL OTHER OPERATING EXPENDITURES			
LIBRARY OPERATIONS	34	$66,370	$3,348
PLANT OPERATION AND MAINTENANCE	35	$51,215	$0
TOTAL ALL OTHER OPERATING EXPENDITURES	36	$120,933	/////
TOTAL OPERATING EXPENDITURES	37	$640,710	/////

PART 2B: LIBRARY CAPITAL EXPENDITURES FROM ALL SOURCES

	LINE NUMBER	AMOUNT
CAPITAL BUDGET EXPENDITURES	38	$28,000

PART 3: LIBRARY STAFF

SECTION A: EMPLOYEES IN FILLED PAID POSITIONS

	Certified Professionals	Total Staff
39 NUMBER OF FULL-TIME, FILLED, PAID POSITIONS	8	18
40 NUMBER OF INDIVIDUALS EMPLOYED PART TIME	1	13
41 FULL TIME EQUIVALENCY OF FILLED, PART-TIME EMPLOYEES	.4	6.6
42 TOTAL FULL-TIME AND PART-TIME EMPLOYEES IN FTE'S	8.4	24.5

SECTION B: BUDGETED POSITIONS VACANT

	Certified Professionals	Total Staff
43 BUDGETED UNFILLED POSITIONS	0	0

PART 4: LIBRARY COLLECTION

	Number of Titles	Number of Volumes
BOOK STOCK		
44 BOOK STOCK OWNED AT START OF YEAR	66,537	78,013
45 PURCHASED IN REPORTING YEAR	4,640	5,425
46 SUPPLIED BY COUNTY LIBRARY ON LONG TERM LOAN	0	0
Gifts Received	200	200
Items Discarded or Returned	450	425
47 OWNED AT END OF YEAR	70,927	83,213
PERIODICALS AND NEWSPAPERS		
48 CURRENT PAID SUBSCRIPTION TITLES	197	
49 NUMBER OF TITLES KEPT 3 OR MORE YEARS	128	
NUMBER OF TITLES INCLUDED IN		
50 STANDARD INDEXES HELD BY YOUR LIBRARY	143	
AUDIOVISUAL AND OTHER NON-PRINT MATERIALS		
51 PURCHASED	304	
52 OWNED, END OF YEAR	2,027	

PART 5: LIBRARY CIRCULATION, INCLUDING LOAN TRANSACTIONS

	To ADULTS	To JUVENILES
53 DIRECT CIRCULATION TO LIBRARY USERS	134,919	70,605
54 RECIPROCAL BORROWING CIRCULATION	3,270	1,684
INTERLIBRARY LOANS		
55 PROVIDED TO OTHER LIBRARIES	96	10
56 RECEIVED FROM OTHER LIBRARIES	110	11
57 BULK LOANS	0	0
58 TOTAL CIRCULATION	210,705	//////
59 STANDARD LOAN PERIOD	21	//////

PART 6: LIBRARY HOURS

	NUMBER
60 TOTAL HOURS PER WEEK MAIN LIBRARY OPEN TO THE PUBLIC	63
61 TOTAL DAYS OPEN PER WEEK	6
EVENINGS PER WEEK MAIN LIBRARY OPEN	
62 TO THE PUBLIC	4
63 WAS THE LIBRARY OPEN SOME WEEKEND HOURS (Yes or No)	Yes

Figure 54. PLSTAT: State Reporting Form for Public Library Statistics, Example Spreadsheet

	A	B	C	D	E	F	G	H	I	J	K	L	M
1	Filename:	PLSTAT											
2	Date Created:												
3	Date Last Changed:												
4													

PUBLIC LIBRARY STATISTICAL REPORT

FILENAME LOCATION YEAR:

PART 1: LIBRARY INCOME

Item	LINE NUMBER	AMOUNT
BALANCE BROUGHT FORWARD	11	24191
LOCAL TAX SUPPORT		
Municipal/County Appropriation	12	474400
Additional Tax Support	13	121729
TOTAL LOCAL TAX SUPPORT	14	L12+L13
CONTRACTUAL	15	0
STATE AID		
Per Capita	16	35490
Other	17	500
TOTAL STATE AID	18	L17+L18
FEDERAL		
LSCA	19	0
Other	20	0
Other	21	0
TOTAL FEDERAL	22	L21+L22+L23
OTHER INCOME	23	26479
TOTAL INCOME	24	L10+L14+L15+L19+L24+L25
CAPITAL BUDGET INCOME	25	20000

PART 2: LIBRARY OPERATING EXPENDITURES FROM ALL SOURCES

Item	LINE NUMBER	AMOUNT Local, Other Funds	AMOUNT Per Capita State Aid
SALARIES AND WAGES	26	336021	33721
FRINGE BENEFITS	27	85548	0
TOTAL PERSONNEL – ALL SOURCES	28	SUM(L35:M36)	/////
MATERIALS			
BOOKS	29	50959	0
PERIODICALS	30	8752	0
AUDIOVISUAL MATERIALS	31	3603	0
OTHER LIBRARY MATERIALS	32	1173	0
TOTAL MATERIALS	33	SUM(L39:M42)	/////
ALL OTHER OPERATING EXPENDITURES			
LIBRARY OPERATIONS	34	66370	3348
PLANT OPERATION AND MAINTENANCE	35	51215	0
TOTAL ALL OTHER OPERATING EXPENDITURES	36	SUM(L45:M46)	/////
TOTAL OPERATING EXPENDITURES	37	L37+L43+L47	

PART 2B: LIBRARY CAPITAL EXPENDITURES FROM ALL SOURCES

Item	LINE NUMBER	AMOUNT
CAPITAL BUDGET EXPENDITURES	38	20000

PART 3: LIBRARY STAFF

SECTION A: EMPLOYEES IN FILLED PAID POSITIONS

	Certified Professionals	Total Staff
NUMBER OF FULL-TIME, FILLED, PAID POSITIONS	8	18
NUMBER OF INDIVIDUALS EMPLOYED PART TIME	1	13
FULL TIME EQUIVALENCY OF FILLED, PART-TIME EMPLOYEES	.4	6.6
TOTAL FULL-TIME AND PART-TIME EMPLOYEES IN FTE'S	8.4	24.5

SECTION B: BUDGETED POSITIONS VACANT

	Certified Professionals	Total Staff
BUDGETED UNFILLED POSITIONS	0	0

PART 4: LIBRARY COLLECTION

	Number of Titles	Number of Volumes
BOOK STOCK		
BOOK STOCK OWNED AT START OF YEAR	66537	78013
PURCHASED IN REPORTING YEAR	4640	5425
SUPPLIED BY COUNTY LIBRARY ON LONG TERM LOAN	0	0
Gifts Received	200	200
Items Discarded or Returned	450	425
OWNED AT END OF YEAR	SUM(L77:L80)-L81	SUM(M77:M80)-M81
PERIODICALS AND NEWSPAPERS		
CURRENT PAID SUBSCRIPTION TITLES	197	
NUMBER OF TITLES KEPT 3 OR MORE YEARS	128	
NUMBER OF TITLES INCLUDED IN STANDARD INDEXES HELD BY YOUR LIBRARY	143	
AUDIOVISUAL AND OTHER NON-PRINT MATERIALS		
PURCHASED	304	
OWNED, END OF YEAR	2027	

PART 5: LIBRARY CIRCULATION, INCLUDING LOAN TRANSACTIONS

	To ADULTS	To JUVENILES
DIRECT CIRCULATION TO LIBRARY USERS	134919	70605
RECIPROCAL BORROWING CIRCULATION	3270	1684
INTERLIBRARY LOANS		
PROVIDED TO OTHER LIBRARIES	96	10
RECEIVED FROM OTHER LIBRARIES	110	11
BULK LOANS	0	0
TOTAL CIRCULATION	SUM(L96:M101)	
STANDARD LOAN PERIOD	21	

PART 6: LIBRARY HOURS

	NUMBER
TOTAL HOURS PER WEEK MAIN LIBRARY OPEN TO THE PUBLIC	63
TOTAL DAYS OPEN PER WEEK	6
EVENINGS PER WEEK MAIN LIBRARY OPEN TO THE PUBLIC	4
WAS THE LIBRARY OPEN SOME WEEKEND HOURS (Yes or No)	Yes

Figure 55. PLSTAT: State Reporting Form for Public Library Statistics, Formula Worksheet

	A	B	C	D	E	F	G	H	I	J
1	Filename:									
2	Date Created:									
3	Date Last Changed:									
4	===									
5										
6	FILENAME	LOCATION	ARL STATISTICS QUESTIONNAIRE YEAR:			1983	1984	1985	1986	1987
7	---									
8										
9			COLLECTIONS							
10			1. Volumes held June 30,			15,236,798				
11			2. Volumes added during year – gross			23,158				
12			3. Volumes withdrawn during year			12,658				
13			4. Volumes added during year – Net			10,500				
14			5. Volumes held June 30,			15,247,298				
15			6. Number of current serials,							
16			including periodicals, received			5,269				
17			7. Reels of microfilm held June 30,			10,236				
18			8. Number of microcards held June 30,			23,369				
19			9. Number of microprint sheets held June 30			2,369				
20			10. Number of microfiche sheets held June 30,			1,125				
21			11. Total microform units held June 30			37,099				
22										
23			PERSONNEL							
24										
25			12. Number of professional staff, FTE			42				
26			13. Number of nonprofessional staff, FTE			125				
27			14. Number of student assistants, FTE			39				
28			15. Total FTE staff			206				
29										
30			INTERLIBRARY LOANS							
31										
32			16. Items loaned:							
33			Originals			659				
34			Photocopies			1,598				
35			Total			2,257				
36			17. Items borrowed:							
37			Originals			123				
38			Photocopies			269				
39			Total			392				
40										

	A	B	C	D	E	F	G	H	I	J
41			EXPENDITURES							
42										
43			18. Books, serials and other library materials			$2,369,874.00				
44			19. Current serials including periodicals			$128,369.00				
45			20. Binding			$51,269.00				
46			21. Total library materials and binding			$2,421,143.00				
47			22. Total salaries and wages, including							
48			student assistants' wages			$569,874.00				
49			23. Other operating expenditures			$259,874.00				
50			24. Total library expenditures			$3,250,891.00				
51			25. Total university educational and							
52			general expenditures			$52,478,698.00				
53			26. Library expenditures as percent of							
54			university expenditures			6.19%				
55										
56			PH.D. DEGREES							
57										
58			27. Number of Ph.D.s awarded			234				
59			28. Number of fields in which Ph.D.s can be awarded			24				
60										
61			ENROLLMENT - FALL							
62										
63			29. Total full-time students			15,269				
64			30. Total FTE part-time students			1,369				
65			31. Total full-time graduate students			859				
66			32. Total FTE part-time graduate students			125				

Figure 56. ARLSTAT: Annual ARL Statistical Report, Example Spreadsheet

	A	B	C	D	E	F	G	H	I	J
1	Filename:									
2	Date Created:									
3	Date Last Changed:									
4	===									
5			ARL STATISTICS QUESTIONNAIRE							
6	FILENAME	LOCATION	ARLSTAT	YEAR:		1983	1984	1985	1986	1987
7	---									
8			COLLECTIONS							
9										
10			1. Volumes held June 30,			15236798				
11			2. Volumes added during year – gross			23158				
12			3. Volumes withdrawn during year			12658				
13			4. Volumes added during year – Net			F11–F12				
14			5. Volumes held June 30,			F10+F13				
15			6. Number of current serials,							
16			including periodicals, received			5269				
17			7. Reels of microfilm held June 30,			10236				
18			8. Number of microcards held June 30,			23369				
19			9. Number of microprint sheets held June 30			2369				
20			10. Number of microfiche sheets held June 30,			1125				
21			11. Total microform units held June 30			SUM(F17:F20)				
22										
23			PERSONNEL							
24										
25			12. Number of professional staff, FTE			42				
26			13. Number of nonprofessional staff, FTE			125				
27			14. Number of student assistants, FTE			39				
28			15. Total FTE staff			SUM(F25:F27)				
29										
30			INTERLIBRARY LOANS							
31										
32			16. Items loaned:							
33			Originals			659				
34			Photocopies			1598				
35			Total			F33+F34				
36										
37			17. Items borrowed:			123				
38			Originals			269				
39			Photocopies			F37+F38				
40			Total							

	A	B	C	D	E	F	G	H	I	J
41			EXPENDITURES							
42										
43			18. Books, serials and other library materials			2369874				
44			19. Current serials including periodicals			128369				
45			20. Binding			51269				
46			21. Total library materials and binding			F43+F45				
47			22. Total salaries and wages, including							
48			student assistants' wages			569874				
49			23. Other operating expenditures			259874				
50			24. Total library expenditures			SUM(F46,F48,F49)				
51			25. Total university educational and							
52			general expenditures			52478698				
53			26. Library expenditures as percent of							
54			university expenditures			F50/F52				
55										
56			PH.D. DEGREES							
57										
58			27. Number of Ph.D.s awarded			234				
59			28. Number of fields in which Ph.D.s can be awarded			24				
60										
61			ENROLLMENT – FALL							
62										
63			29. Total full-time students			15269				
64			30. Total FTE part-time students			1369				
65			31. Total full-time graduate students			859				
66			32. Total FTE part-time graduate students			125				

Figure 57. ARLSTAT: Annual ARL Statistical Report, Formula Worksheet

Using the Model

Unless you are a New Jersey public librarian, this spreadsheet must be modified to reflect your state's reporting system. The main thing to remember is to include enough space to record the filename where each piece of data is recorded and the exact location of the data on that file. If you do this, you will not have to search through many files to find the information when you prepare your report.

ARLSTAT: A Model for Assembling the Annual Association for Research Libraries Statistical Report

The ARLSTAT spreadsheet (figure 56) is similar to the HEGIS and PLSTAT spreadsheets in that it is primarily a reporting form placed on a spreadsheet. As noted earlier in the discussion of HEGIS and PLSTAT, this is a convenient way to keep a record of the location of the relevant pieces of information found in your files.

In addition to assembling annual data, the spreadsheet can be expanded to include data from past years or to enter the same data next year and for years after. If you do this for a number of years, you can analyze trends over time, using the CORREG spreadsheet. In fact, you should have enough space on this spreadsheet to copy the entire CORREG spreadsheet to the bottom portion of this spreadsheet, thus saving you time in transferring data from one file to another.

The spreadsheet itself is not complicated. The descriptive text is located in columns C and D. The data and the few simple summation formulas are entered in column F. (See figure 57.)

3 Warm-Up Exercises for the Occasional Spreadsheet User

If you are just starting to learn how to use a spreadsheet program or are only an occasional user, these exercises will allow you to practice certain basic operations that take place when designing a spreadsheet. For the most part, each should take just a few minutes to perform, once you have gone through them a few times. Admittedly, the first few times through will take some work, but afterward they should fulfill their intended purpose: to get you "warmed up" or to review a particular operation.

Use the Command Comparison Guide in the first section along with your program's Reference Guide, to find the exact keystrokes to perform the operations called for in each exercise. Space has been provided to allow you to write in these sequences for your spreadsheet. This also yields a brief reference guide for you to use later.

In my observations of people who do not use a spreadsheet program every day or very frequently, I have noticed that the most difficult operation to perform is the REPLICATE or COPY function. Warm-Up Exercise 4 is thus very important to both learn and practice.

Exercise 8 drills you in modifying a spreadsheet, particularly in adding additional rows and columns. You will find that you need to know how to do this when you try to modify the spreadsheets I have given as examples in this book.

Finally, the exercise on saving and loading (no. 7) must be done with your program's Reference Guide in hand. This operation differs so much from spreadsheet program to program that it is difficult to give firm guidance, except to refer you to your program's instructions.

Exercise **1**:
Cursor Movement

Functions Reviewed

UP, DOWN, RIGHT,
LEFT
GOTO Command
Spreadsheet Commands

The first thing you must learn is how to move the cursor around the spreadsheet. This exercise also gets your fingers loosened and your mind into the structure of the spreadsheet. Do the following, using the arrow keys.

1. Start at cell A1. Move to A10.
2. Move to F10.
3. Move to F1.
4. Return to A1.
5. Move to C5.
6. Return to A1.

Do the entire sequence, using the GOTO command.

You now know how to get back to "home base," or cell A1. Be adventurous and move to the following:

Z56, then
H8, then
A240, then
back home, A1

Move the cursor to the bottom lower-right of the spreadsheet.

You can use the arrow keys, but try to do it with the GOTO command as well. Then retreat back home.

Exercise **2**:
Entering Numbers and Text

Functions Reviewed

Number Entry,
Label (Text) Entry,
Editing the Entry Line
Spreadsheet Commands

There is a difference between entering numbers that you may wish to calculate and entering text (such as the name of your library). Numbers are referred to as *values* and text is referred to as *labels* in some spreadsheet instructions. This exercise makes sure you know which is which.

1. Enter the number 123 in cell A1.
2. Enter the number 456 in cell A2.
3. Enter the number 789 in cell A3.
4. Enter your first name in cell B1.
5. Enter the word LOVES in cell B2.
6. Enter the word BOOKS in cell B3.
7. Overwrite LOVES with HATES in cell B2.
8. Overwrite 789 with 101 in cell A3.

Practice editing some text that you enter before you hit the return key. Find out how to move the cursor around the entry line and how to add and delete words and letters while on the entry line.

Functions Reviewed

Entering FORMULAS
ADDITION,
SUBTRACTION,
MULTIPLICATION,
DIVISION
The SUM Function
Spreadsheet Commands

Formulas are generally entered like numbers or *values*. However, spreadsheet programs vary in how formulas must be entered. Check your manual, if you are unsure, then do the following.

1. Enter the number 123 in cell A1.
2. Enter the number 456 in cell A2.
3. Enter the number 789 in cell A3.
4. Add the three together in cell A4 by entering A1+A2+A3.
5. Add the three together in cell A5 by entering SUM(A1:A3).
6. Add the three together in cell A6 by entering 123+456+789.
7. Do the numbers in A4, A5, and A6 agree? If not, you have made a mistake.
8. In cell B1, subtract the number in A1 from the number in A3 (A3—A1).
9. In cell B2, multiply A1 by A3 (A1∗A3).
10. In cell B3, divide A3 by A1 (A3/A1).
11. In cell B4, divide 789 by 123. The result should be the same as in cell B3.
12. In cell B5, divide what is in cell A3 by the number 123. The result should be the same as in cells B3 and B4. If not, you have made a mistake.

If you have done everything correctly, here is what your results and your formulas should look like.

Your results should look like:

	A	B
1	123	666
2	456	97047
3	789	6.414634146
4	1368	6.414634146
5	1368	6.414634146
6	1368	

Your formulas should look like:

	A	B
1	123	A3—A1
2	456	A1∗A3
3	789	A3/A1
4	A1+A2+A3	789/123
5	SUM(A1:A3)	A3/123
6	123+456+789	

Exercise **4**:
Replicating and Copying

Functions Reviewed

REPLICATE, COPY
Calculating Percent
Spreadsheet Commands

One of the commands you will use most often throughout this book is the REPLICATE command (sometimes also referred to as the COPY command). Using the REPLICATE command, you will be able to perform two needed functions. First, you will be able to duplicate the contents of one cell to one or more other cells. Second, you will be able to duplicate the contents of many cells to many other cells on the spreadsheet.

First, practice duplicating your name from one cell to other cells by using the REPLICATE command.

1. Enter your first name in cell A1.
2. REPLICATE your name in cell A1 to cell D1, then to D5, then to A15.
3. REPLICATE your name in cell A1 to cells A2 through A10, using a single command.
4. REPLICATE your name in cell A1 to cells C1 through F1.

Second, practice duplicating a range of cells containing your name to another range of cells.

5. REPLICATE all those names in A1 through A10 to B1 through B10, using just one command. (This is sometimes referred to as the COPY command.) This practices replicating down a column.
6. REPLICATE the names in C1 through F1 to C5 through F5. This practices replicating across a row.

Practice until you feel comfortable with these exercises.

The biggest problem you will face is replicating with formulas. You must learn the difference between absolute and relative variables. *Absolute variables* are those cell references you do *not* wish to change. *Relative variables* are those you *want* to change. The problem is that sometimes, in a single formula, you will want some cell references *not* to change (an absolute variable) and you will want other cell references to *change* (a relative variable), as when you wish to calculate a series of percentages. The exercise shows you how this takes place.

First, practice replicating formulas when all the cell references change (i.e., relative variables).

1. Enter the number 1 in cell A1.
2. Enter the formula A1+1 in cell A2.
3. REPLICATE the formula in A2 to A3 through A10.
4. REPLICATE all the formulas from A1 through A10 to cells B1 through B10. You should have the same results as you have in A1 through A10.

Second, practice replicating formulas when one cell reference changes (relative variable) and one does not change (absolute variable). The percentaging problem is an excellent example of this.

5. Find the percentage of each entry in B1 through B10 and place the result in C1 through C10. To do this,
(a) enter the function SUM(B1:B10) in cell B11.

(b) then, in cell C1, divide what is in cell B1 by B11 and multiply by 100: (B1/B11)∗100.

(c) REPLICATE C1 to C2 through C10, but when asked, make B1 "relative" and B11 "no change." The reason is that we are dividing by a constant, the SUM in cell B11, and we do not want that to change.

6. Find the sum of column C and place it in cell C11. This should equal 100.

In some spreadsheet programs, such as Lotus 1-2-3, you may have to place a *special character* in your formula just before the cell reference you do not want to change. Check your manual, especially if you are using Lotus 1-2-3.

Here is what the results and the formulas will look like in your spreadsheet:

	A		B		C	
1 ¦ 1			1		1.818181818	
2 ¦ 2			2		3.636363636	
3 ¦ 3			3		5.454545455	
4 ¦ 4			4		7.272727273	
5 ¦ 5			5		9.090909091	
6 ¦ 6			6		10.90909091	
7 ¦ 7			7		12.72727273	
8 ¦ 8			8		14.54545455	
9 ¦ 9			9		16.36363636	
10 ¦ 10			10		18.18181818	
11 ¦			55		100	

Your formulas should look like this:

	A		B		C	
1 ¦ 1			1		(B1/B11)∗100	
2 ¦ A1+1			B1+1		(B2/B11)∗100	
3 ¦ A2+1			B2+1		(B3/B11)∗100	
4 ¦ A3+1			B3+1		(B4/B11)∗100	
5 ¦ A4+1			B4+1		(B5/B11)∗100	
6 ¦ A5+1			B5+1		(B6/B11)∗100	
7 ¦ A6+1			B6+1		(B7/B11)∗100	
8 ¦ A7+1			B7+1		(B8/B11)∗100	
9 ¦ A8+1			B8+1		(B9/B11)∗100	
10 ¦ A9+1			B9+1		(B10/B11)∗100	
11 ¦			SUM(B1:B10)		SUM(C1:C10)	

Exercise 5:
Formating

Functions Reviewed

Change Column Width
LEFT and RIGHT
Justification
Integer and Dollar/Cents
Display
Spreadsheet Commands

This exercise involves changing column widths, right and left justification of text and numbers, and showing numbers as (a) integers (no decimals) and (b) dollars and cents (2 decimals).

1. Enter the word LIBRARIANS in cell A1.
2. Enter the words SIMPLY ADORE in cell A2.
3. Enter the words PRINTED MATERIAL in cell A3.
4. Enter the number 12345 in cell B1.
5. Enter the number 67890 in cell B2.
6. Enter the number 54321 in cell B3.

If your column width is set at 9, you will probably see this:

	A		B
1	LIBRARIAN		12345
2	SIMPLY AD		67890
3	PRINTED M		54321

7. Use the FORMAT command to change the column widths to 12. Now the phrase PRINTED MATERIAL looks like this: PRINTED MATE.
8. Use the FORMAT command to change the column widths to 16. Now everything should show on the screen.
9. Use the FORMAT command to "right justify" the text, and you should see this:

	A		B
1	LIBRARIANS		12345
2	SIMPLY ADORE		67890
3	PRINTED MATERIAL		54321

10. Change cell B1 to 123.45.
11. Change cell B2 to 6.7890.
12. FORMAT ROW 1 to integer.
13. FORMAT ROW 2 to $ (the dollar-and-cents format) and this is what you should see:

	A		B
1	LIBRARIANS		123
2	SIMPLY ADORE		6.79
3	PRINTED MATERIAL		54321

14. Now try to get everything to look as it did when you first entered the information. You will have to change the column widths, left-justify the columns, edit the number cells to remove the decimals, and change integer and $ to the general format, etc. Use just the commands and do not reenter the information. You should get a spreadsheet like this:

```
    |      A       ::        B        |
1 |      LIBRARIAN          12345
2 |      SIMPLY AD          67890
3 |      PRINTED M          54321
```

Exercise **6**: Inserting and Moving

Functions Reviewed

INSERT, DELETE, MOVE
Spreadsheet Commands

Occasionally you will want to insert or delete a column or a row, or move a column or a row from one place to another. In the following, set the width of all columns to 12.

1. Enter "Fiction" in cell A1.
2. Enter "Nonfiction" in cell A2.
3. Enter "AV Material" in cell A3.
4. Enter "Total" in cell A4.
5. Enter 1234 in cell B1.
6. Enter 5678 in cell B2.
7. Enter 212 in cell B3.
8. Sum B1 through B3 in cell B4.
9. INSERT a new ROW 4 to make a blank space between "AV Material" and "Total."
10. INSERT a new COLUMN B.

Your spreadsheet should now look like this:

```
    |      A       ::        B       ::        C       |
1 | Fiction                                    1234
2 | Nonfiction                                 5678
3 | AV Material                                 212
4 |
5 | Total                                      7124
```

11. DELETE column B.
12. DELETE row 4.
13. MOVE column B to column E.
14. MOVE row 4 to row 6.

Practice inserting, deleting, and moving with this spreadsheet.

Exercise **7**: Storing and Loading

Functions Reviewed

STORE (SAVE),
LOAD (READ)
Spreadsheet Commands

You will want to STORE the text, numbers, and formulas that you enter so that you can retrieve them later (through the LOAD command). The first series of exercises deals with simple storage and loading. The second series of exercises deals with saving and loading only a part of the spreadsheet. Often, you will want to load only a total column from one spreadsheet into a new spreadsheet, or store only part of a spreadsheet. Initially, you will have to *follow your instructional manual very closely* in order to complete the exercise satisfactorily.

Simple Storing and Loading

Set column width to 12.

1. Enter Fiction in cell A1.
2. Enter Nonfiction in cell A2.
3. Enter AV Material in cell A3.
4. Enter Total in cell A4.
5. Enter 1234 in cell B1.
6. Enter 5678 in cell B2.
7. Enter 212 in cell B3.
8. Sum B1 through B3 in cell B4.
9. STORE entire contents of the spreadsheet into a file named MARCH.
10. Use the CLEAR command to erase everything on the spreadsheet.
11. LOAD the file named MARCH.

Your spreadsheet should look like this.

	A	B
1	Fiction	1234
2	Nonfiction	5678
3	AV Material	212
4	Total	7124

12. Use the CLEAR command to erase everything on the spreadsheet.

Partial Storing and Loading

Spreadsheet programs vary greatly in the ease they afford for saving and loading partial contents of one spreadsheet into another. In my experience, VisiCalc presents the most difficulties and Multiplan and other newer spreadsheet programs are the easiest to use in this regard.

Here is a typical problem you might have to solve, in which you must move the partial contents of one spreadsheet into another spreadsheet. The file MARCH, which we just created, is a summary of March circulation for your library. You may want to take that information and transfer it to a new spreadsheet that we will call YEAR. It looks like this:

	A	B	C	D
1	Categories	January	February	March
2				
3	Fiction	2233	3333	
4	Nonfiction	4444	5555	
5	AV Material	111	222	
6	Total	6788	9110	

This is a month-by-month summary that you are accumulating for the year. You want to transfer the March figures to their appropriate column on the YEAR spreadsheet. You do not want to copy the categories in column A, because they are already there. You just want to transfer column B in the file MARCH to column D in the file YEAR. In other words, you want your updated spreadsheet to look like this:

	A	B	C	D
1	Categories	January	February	March
2				
3	Fiction	2233	3333	1234
4	Nonfiction	4444	5555	5678
5	AV Material	111	222	212
6	Total	6788	9110	7124

In some spreadsheet programs, you can simply enter a command that transfers the information in column B of MARCH to column D of YEAR. That's a very nice feature.

However, if such a transfer is not as easily performed, you may have to follow a procedure like the following.

1. Place the cursor at the upper left portion of the area you wish to save.
2. STORE the spreadsheet into a DIF (Data Interchange Format) file.
3. When prompted, specify the lower-right corner of the area you wish to save.
4. The file is now stored.
5. CLEAR the screen.
6. LOAD the new spreadsheet you are working on (e.g., YEAR).
7. Place the cursor where you want to LOAD the information from the DIF file.
8. Enter the command LOAD with the DIF filename.
9. The data should be entered in the designated area.

You will notice that, with this procedure, formulas such as SUM will not be transferred. You must re-SUM the column on the new worksheet.

As an exercise,

.

Create the file YEAR
Transfer the information in column B of MARCH to column D of YEAR
STORE your revised YEAR file, to access later

Practice this transfer often, because many spreadsheets in this book require this procedure.

Exercise 8:
Modifying Spreadsheets

Functions Reviewed

Inserting, Moving,
Editing Formulas
Spreadsheet Commands

You will have to modify many of the spreadsheet examples in this book because the categories you use are not the same as those that I use. Further, you may have a need for a larger spreadsheet than I provide. This warm-up exercise is designed to help you increase the size of a spreadsheet.

If you have saved the spreadsheet YEAR from Warm-Up Exercise 7, load it into your program. If not, create that spreadsheet and save it so you have a copy.

Here's YEAR:

	A	B	C	D
1	Categories	January	February	March
2				
3	Fiction	2233	3333	1234
4	Nonfiction	4444	5555	5678
5	AV Material	111	222	212
6	Total	6788	9110	7124

Add the following formulas to the spreadsheet in column E, as shown on this example.

	A	B	C	D	E
1	Categories	January	February	March	Total
2					
3	Fiction	2233	3333	1234	SUM(B3:D3)
4	Nonfiction	4444	5555	5678	SUM(B4:D4)
5	AV Material	111	222	212	SUM(B5:D5)
6	Total	6788	9110	7124	SUM(B6:D6)

Your problem is to insert nine more months of data into this spreadsheet in columns E through M and have the total in column N.

1. MOVE column E to column N, using the MOVE command. If you do not have a MOVE command or something that moves a column or row from one place to another, try REPLICATING or COPYING column E to column N.
2. Change the first SUM formula in cell N3 from SUM(B3:D3) to SUM(B3:N3).
3. REPLICATE the formula in cells N3 to N4 through N6.

You can use the same technique if you want to add additional rows to your spreadsheet. Just move the formulas that are in a given row to a lower portion of your spreadsheet, change the last row reference in your formula to match the new size of the spreadsheet, and you are ready to proceed.

Decreasing the size of a spreadsheet is usually much simpler. Just delete the rows you do not want and the formulas will adjust to the smaller size. Therefore, if you have the space, enter extra rows or columns before your formula rows or columns, and delete them when you are sure your design is set.

Index

Philip M. Clark is an associate professor in the Division of Library and Information Science at St. John's University in Jamaica, New York. He was formerly director of the Montclair (N.J.) Public Library, and is active in the American Library Association, the New Jersey Library Association and the Association for Library and Information Science Education. He has directed several research projects focusing on public libraries and has contributed to numerous journals.